W9-AXF-298

681.113
W68c
96921
DATE DUE
WITHDRAWN
L. R. COLLEGE LIBRARY

CLOCKS & WATCHES

Johann Willsberger

CLOCKS & WATCHES

SIX HUNDRED YEARS OF THE WORLD'S MOST BEAUTIFUL TIMEPIECES

Introduction by

Arnold Toynbee

Translation by Renée Vera Cafiero

The Dial Press
New York
1975

Library of Congress Cataloging in Publication Data

Willsberger, Johann, 1941–
Clocks and watches.

Translation of Zauberhafte Gehäuse der Zeit.
1. Clocks and watches. I. Title.
NK7485.W44413 681′.113 74-28148
ISBN 0-8037-4475-7

Manufactured in the Federal Republic of Germany

First printing, 1975

Clocks and Watches: Symbols of Our Modern Way of Life

Arnold Toynbee

Clocks and watches are indispensable instruments for the conduct of modern life. Airplanes, passenger railway trains, omnibuses, and passenger ships have exact times for departing and arriving. These times are measured in terms of the position of the moving pointers on the dial of a clock or watch. The figures of the hours and minutes that are indicated on the dial are published in timetables, and the authorities that are responsible for operating these various means of conveyance pride themselves (except when they are on strike) on carrying out their timetables as accurately as they can. A would-be passenger who does not obey the timetable is likely to miss the conveyance in which he is intending to travel.

An apparent liberation from the tyranny of having to conform to timetables is one of the attractions of possessing a private automobile of one's own; but this liberation is not complete unless the owner-driver of the car makes the whole journey in his own car from start to finish. If he has to make part of his journey by public transport, he is still at the mercy of a timetable. Today there is a bridge for automobiles across the Bosphorus, but there is not yet either a bridge or a tunnel over or under the Atlantic Ocean, or even over or under the Straits of Gibraltar, the Straits of Dover, or across the Behring Sea. For a journey all round the globe, a motorist is not yet free to "take his own time."

"Clocking in" and "clocking out" are part of the necessary discipline of work in factories and offices, and this is the kind of work by which an increasing percentage of the world's working population is earning its living. The exact numbers of hours and minutes of working time, and the exact moments for starting and stopping work and for breaks are nowadays the subjects of meticulous and stubborn collective bargaining. If these figures were not agreed in terms of clock-time, the conduct of the world's business would fall into chaos; neither wages nor profits could be earned. In schools the hours of attendance are just as strictly regulated and enforced, and so they are too in sports and games. The winning or losing of a football match may turn on the accuracy of the reckoning of half time and of the moment for the close of play. In sports that are competitions in speed, the time taken by the competitors to complete the course is recorded with minute accuracy; account is taken even of fractions of seconds.

The times fixed with doctors or dentists for appointments have to be kept punctiliously by the patient; otherwise, he may lose the practitioner's service. In countries in which there is trial by jury, a juryman who fails to present himself, or who arrives late, may incur serious penalties. A traveller in Australia or New Zealand finds a notice on the doors of hotel-restaurants: "Service in this restaurant ends at such-and-such an hour sharp." The word "sharp" is underlined, and if the traveller does present himself one minute later than the advertised closing time, he will have to go hungry till the advertised opening time on the following morning.

The liturgy of the Christian church presupposes an ability to tell the successive times of day, and so does the obligation, incumbent on Muslims, to say their prayers five times in every twenty-four hours. Nowadays the correct hours can be ascertained by the use of clocks; but, for centuries before the invention of clocks, the hours for worship were indicated to the congregation by the fiat of the ecclesiastical authorities. In Western Christendom the canonical hour was and still is announced by the ringing of bells; in the Islamic world it was (and still is) announced by a vocal call to prayer. In the Islamic world there is an annual fast in daylight hours which lasts from one new moon to the next. Nowadays, the exact moments of the beginnings and endings of lunar months are known and could be announced; but the official beginnings and endings of the Islamic fasting month Ramadan are not ascertained by astronomical calculations and are not proclaimed in terms of clock-time. They are determined by the moment at which an ecclesiastical authority announces that he has first seen the new moon. Authoritative observation, not scientific reckoning, is decisive.

Observation of the heavenly bodies may be official, but it is, of course, a method of telling the time that is subject to considerable error. It depends on the eyesight and the honesty of the observer. It also depends on the state of the weather. The sun and the stars may be hidden by fog or by clouds. A great-uncle of mine, who was the commander of one of the British East India Company's sailing ships, became noted for the accuracy of his observations in difficult circumstances. Accordingly, when the British Government established a meteorological office in London, my great-uncle was invited to join the staff. He therefore retired from service at sea in the year 1866. He had never commanded a steamship.

In my great-uncle's old age, his most precious possessions were the chronometers which he had used for his navigation. Why did a seaman who was good at taking observations of the sun and the stars need clocks as well? The reason was that observations of the heavenly bodies suffice, by themselves, for ascertaining a ship's latitude, but not for ascertaining its longitude. The ascertainment of longitude, too, became important when, at the close of the fifteenth century, ships began to sail from the Atlantic coasts of Europe eastward and westward to the opposite side of the globe. For more than two centuries after that, navigators used to guess the longitude of their ships' successive positions by the rough-and-ready method of "dead reckoning"—i.e., by estimating the distance that they had traversed, eastward or westward, day by day since the first day of the voyage. It was eventually realized that a ship's position in terms of longitude could be fixed exactly by measuring the difference between the time of day in that position, as ascertained by observation at the moment, and the time at the same moment at the ship's point of departure, as measured by a clock that told the time in terms of time at the departure point.

This, however, could not be done until a chronometer had been invented that was capable, when once it had been set going, of keeping time accurately for months on end. Complete accuracy was needed, for an error of even a few seconds in the indication of time on the chronometer would generate an appreciable error in the calculation of the longitude of the ship's position when this position was deduced from a comparison of the chronometer's reading with the navigator's observations. In 1714 the British Government offered the at that date princely monetary reward of £20,000 to anyone who succeeded in manufacturing a chronometer that would keep time accurately enough to fulfill the exacting requirements for the precise ascertainment of a ship's longitude.

This prize was awarded in 1762 to John Harrison. That date marks the beginning of a new epoch, not only in the history of navigation, but in the recognition of the differences in time zones and in the metaphysical conception of time itself. Time changes in ratio with changes in longitude. A day's journey westward makes that day longer; a day's journey eastward makes that day shorter. If we travel latitudinally round the globe from our starting point, we lose one whole day if we are going from east to west, and we gain one whole day if we are going in the opposite direction. In 1884 an imaginary "date-line" was drawn longitudinally on the map of the Pacific Ocean, and voyagers who cross this line add or subtract one day in their calendar according to the direction in which they are travelling.

When we travel by airplane even for a shorter distance latitudinally, we feel the change of time both physically and psychologically. At this speed of travel, the change of time is sudden enough to be upsetting. It is the speed that makes the difference. In 1929 I travelled from Vladivostok to Moscow by train. The journey took a week, because the Russians and the Chinese had been fighting each other in Manchuria, so the Russian transcontinental train could not take the Manchurian short cut. At the principal stations en route, two clocks stood side by side, one of them showing local time and the other showing simultaneous Moscow time. In Eastern Siberia, the discrepancy between the two times was great enough to be intellectually striking, but the speed of travel was not great enough to cause physical or psychological discomfort, though the direction was latitudinal and the journey was long.

The clocks in Siberia that showed Moscow time were counterparts of my great-uncle's chronometers, and the image of his chronometers is printed sharply on my visual memory, because one day, when I was a child, the cat knocked those delicate instruments over, and my uncle accused me, mistakenly but wrathfully, of having committed this act of vandalism. A chronometer is a chef-d'oeuvre of the art of making time-recording instruments, but the need for recording time was felt, and cruder instruments for recording it were invented, long before the year 1714. The Christians' and Muslims' need for ascertaining and announcing the canonical hours of prayer has been mentioned already. Earlier still, the Athenians found it necessary to ration the amount of time allowed to a speaker in their public assembly, and for this purpose they invented the klepsydra. This was an instrument that worked on the same principle as the more recent hour-glass, with the difference that, in the klepsydra, water performed the function that, in an hour-glass, is performed by sand. In the klepsydra, a quantum of water was transferred by force of gravity from one container to another through a pipe of a diameter that made this amount of water take a particular limited length of time to transfer itself from the upper container to the lower one.

It is no accident that more accurate timekeepers than the klepsydra and the hour-glass were invented in the late Middle Ages in the rising commercial industrial cities of northern Europe. North of the Alps, busy people cannot count on being able to tell the time by observing the position of the sun; for here, as often as not, the sun is hidden by clouds, while here, by the fourteenth century, it had already be come true, for workers in factories and offices, that "time is money." Time is not money for cultivators of the soil or for shepherds and herdsmen, because the speed at which they work is not under their own control. The pace of their work is dictated to them by the climatic rhythm of the seasons and by the physiological rhythm of sowing-time, reaping-time, milking-time, lambing-time, and calving-time. Late medieval urban trade and manufacture evoked the demand for clocks; early modern oceanic navigation evoked the demand for clocks of the chronometer's standard of accuracy.

However, the need to tell the time and to be punctual was not felt by very many people, anywhere in the world, till quite recently, and owning a watch of one's own is not a much older requirement than owning an automobile of one's own. I am still occasionally stopped and asked what the time is by someone who does not wear a watch. When I was a child in London, one could ascertain the time readily without wearing a watch and without asking a passer-by, because many shops had a clock. This was placed just above the notice that gave the shopkeeper's name and the description of the kind of goods that he had for sale, and, in an age in which potential customers did not wear watches, this was an effective means of advertising. On looking at the clock to learn the time, the passer-by also learnt the shopkeeper's name and the nature of his stock of wares. In 1925 I visited the United States for the first time, and I noticed that, in New York, in contrast to London, clocks on shop-fronts were rare. I guessed that this was because, by 1925, most Americans did wear watches. They were rich enough to buy them, and they did buy them and use them because they were more acutely conscious than even their British contemporaries were that "time is money."

As recently as the early years of the twentieth century, time was not money in Albania. The Albanians' way of time-keeping is described by an English observer, Edith Durham, who travelled in Albania at that date. The way was as simple as the birds' way. The Albanians went to bed at dusk, and they got up at dawn, without regard to the seasonal variation in the respective durations of darkness and daylight—in spite of the fact that Albania lies far enough away from the Equator for the seasonal variation there to be considerable.

Long before that date, in many parts of the world, daytime and nighttime had each been divided into twelve hours; but, like the twentieth-century Albanians' day and night, these hours originally varied seasonally in length. It was only at the equinoxes that all the twenty-four hours in a day and a night were of equal length. Moreover, hours could not be timed at all precisely before the invention of clocks. The Athenians devised the klepsydra, but in general they were vague in their indications of the time of day. "When the market-place is crowded" was an Athenian designation for one time of day, and, for modern people, this vagueness is surprising.

During all but the latest age of human history, the sun has served mankind as its clock. On the Equator the sun is an accurate time indicator. Here, year in and year out, the sun rises suddenly and exactly at 6 A.M., it is at its zenith exactly at noon, and it sets suddenly and exactly at 6 P.M. By contrast, within the Arctic and Antarctic circles, the sun-clock fails to work both when there are twenty-four hours of continuous darkness and when there are twenty-four hours of continuous light in each day-and-night period.

Outside the Arctic and Antarctic circles, it was possible to give the sun-clock greater precision by the use of a sundial. The shadows cast by the dial's indicator (called *gnomon* in Greek) did indicate, more

Erratum

Page 6 of the Introduction is a repeat of page 5. No material has been left out of the Introduction, and we regret the error.

or less accurately, the seasonally varying lengths of the daylight hours, though it could not indicate these when the sun was obscured by clouds and it could give no indication whatsoever of the hours between sunset and sunrise.

To us moderns who are equipped with chronometers, the sundial seems a crude instrument, yet, in the third century B.C., an eminent Greek man of science, Eratosthenes, used a pair of sundials for measuring the circumference of the planet Earth, and his estimate of its length came remarkably close to the true figure. Eratosthenes set up one of his sundials at Alexandria and the other at Aswan (Syene), and he knew that Aswan was nearly due south of Alexandria and that it was approximately 5,000 stadia distant from it. He found that, at the summer solstice, the indicator of his sundial at Aswan cast no shadow at all, whereas, at the same moment, the indicator of his sundial at Alexandria did cast a shadow which could, of course, be measured. Eratosthenes now had two figures at his service: the figure for the distance between Alexandria and Aswan, and the figure for the length of the shadow cast by the sundial at Alexandria at the summer solstice. The ratio of the length of the shadow cast by the indicator of the sundial at Alexandria on that day to the length of the distance between Alexandria and Aswan gave Eratosthenes his clue for estimating the length of the circumference of the earth. By present-day standards, Eratosthenes's instrument was primitive; but Eratosthenes's intellect was a match for the intellect of any modern scientist. His intellectual ability enabled him to use his primitive instrument for making a sophisticated calculation.

A concern for punctuality is an eighteenth-century British innovation. This preceded the Industrial Revolution, and it was one of the enabling conditions that made this revolution practicable.

Goethe, in his *Italienische Reise,* gives an entertaining account of an encounter of his with this novel British fad. At Naples in the year 1787, Goethe received a message to the following effect from an English nobleman: "Mr. Goethe, people tell me that you are quite famous. I want to meet you. Kindly come to the cathedral at such-and-such an hour on such-and-such a day; you will find me on the steps outside, and I can give you ten minutes of my time." Goethe might reasonably have taken umbrage. By 1787 he was in truth world famous already. However, he was intrigued by the Englishman's quaint combination of arrogance, naïveté, and meticulousness about time-keeping, so Goethe decided to accept the appointment that the Englishman had dictated to him. As Goethe approached the cathedral, there, sure enough, was the Englishman standing on the steps, holding his watch in his hand (wristwatches had not then been invented). Continuing to hold his watch, the Englishman talked to Goethe for exactly ten minutes. When the time was up, he broke the conversation off. "I must be in time," he said, "for my next appointment," and, to keep this appointment, he parted company with Goethe abruptly. Goethe was amused. On this occasion he did not realize, as he did, later on, on the evening after the Battle of Valmy, that he was witnessing the end of one epoch and the beginning of another. Actually the British Industrial Revolution has influenced mankind's destiny more profoundly than the French political Revolution.

What was it that had made that English nobleman more fussy about time than his famous German contemporary Goethe was? The English nobleman's or less accurately, the seasonally varying lengths of the daylight hours, though it could not indicate these when the sun was obscured by clouds and it could give no indication whatsoever of the hours between sunset and sunrise.

To us moderns who are equipped with chronometers, the sundial seems a crude instrument, yet, in the third century B.C., an eminent Greek man of science, Eratosthenes, used a pair of sundials for measuring the circumference of the planet Earth, and his estimate of its length came remarkably close to the true figure. Eratosthenes set up one of his sundials at Alexandria and the other at Aswan (Syene), and he knew that Aswan was nearly due south of Alexandria and that it was approximately 5,000 stadia distant from it. He found that, at the summer solstice, the indicator of his sundial at Aswan cast no shadow at all, whereas, at the same moment, the indicator of his sundial at Alexandria did cast a shadow which could, of course, be measured. Eratosthenes now had two figures at his service: the figure for the distance between Alexandria and Aswan, and the figure for the length of the shadow cast by the sundial at Alexandria at the summer solstice. The ratio of the length of the shadow cast by the indicator of the sundial at Alexandria on that day to the length of the distance between Alexandria and Aswan gave Eratosthenes his clue for estimating the length of the circumference of the earth. By present-day standards, Eratosthenes's instrument was primitive; but Eratosthenes's intellect was a match for the intellect of any modern scientist. His intellectual ability enabled him to use his primitive instrument for making a sophisticated calculation.

A concern for punctuality is an eighteenth-century British innovation. This preceded the Industrial Revolution, and it was one of the enabling conditions that made this revolution practicable.

Goethe, in his *Italienische Reise,* gives an entertaining account of an encounter of his with this novel British fad. At Naples in the year 1787, Goethe received a message to the following effect from an English nobleman: "Mr. Goethe, people tell me that you are quite famous. I want to meet you. Kindly come to the cathedral at such-and-such an hour on such-and-such a day; you will find me on the steps outside, and I can give you ten minutes of my time." Goethe might reasonably have taken umbrage. By 1787 he was in truth world famous already. However, he was intrigued by the Englishman's quaint combination of arrogance, naïveté, and meticulousness about time-keeping, so Goethe decided to accept the appointment that the Englishman had dictated to him. As Goethe approached the cathedral, there, sure enough, was the Englishman standing on the steps, holding his watch in his hand (wristwatches had not then been invented). Continuing to hold his watch, the Englishman talked to Goethe for exactly ten minutes. When the time was up, he broke the conversation off. "I must be in time," he said, "for my next appointment," and, to keep this appointment, he parted company with Goethe abruptly. Goethe was amused. On this occasion he did not realize, as he did, later on, on the evening after the Battle of Valmy, that he was witnessing the end of one epoch and the beginning of another. Actually the British Industrial Revolution has influenced mankind's destiny more profoundly than the French political Revolution.

What was it that had made that English nobleman more fussy about time than his famous German contemporary Goethe was? The English nobleman's time-consciousness was surely a product of the stagecoach. In 1787, roads in Britain were not yet macadamised, and they were infested with highwaymen. Consequently, stagecoaches did not yet keep to their scheduled time as accurately as they did half a century later, when they were on the point of being put out of action by railway trains. Probably the English nobleman had never travelled in a stagecoach himself; he is more likely to have travelled in a private coach of his own, escorted by a sufficient number of armed outriders to deter the highwaymen from trying to waylay him. All the same, in Britain by the year 1787, stagecoach timetables were already precise enough, and were sufficiently accurately carried out, to make punctuality psychologically obligatory, even for an English nobleman.

In English literature there are two well-known accounts of a journey by stagecoach. One is by Charles Dickens in *A Tale of Two Cities,* and this fictional journey by coach is dated by Dickens to the time of the French Revolution. The second account is by a less well-known British author, Thomas Hughes, in a book called *Tom Brown's Schooldays.* This second account is semi-autobiographical, and it describes a genuine journey that was made by the author, when he was a schoolboy, rather less than half a century later than the imaginary date of the fictional coach journey described by Dickens. The difference between these two accounts is very striking. In the fictional coach journey at the time of the French Revolution, the "guard" fills up the "boot" of the coach with loaded fire-arms, and the psychological atmosphere in which the journey starts is a sense of fear. In "Tom Brown's" coach less than fifty years later there is still a guard, but he carries no weapons. There is no longer any question of the journey being dangerous. The features of the journey that fascinate the schoolboy traveller are the coach's speed and its punctuality. By this date, the time sense that is characteristic of the Age of Mechanization is already fully developed, though Tom Brown's coach is still drawn by horses. Before this book comes to an end, Tom describes a later journey that he made—this time in one of the "coaches" in a train drawn along rails by a steam-driven locomotive. Down to the present day, the official who commands a railway train is still called "the guard" in Britain. Perhaps the time will come when the guard will, once again, be armed as heavily as he was in the seventeen-nineties. In 1974, the tide of lawless violence is rising again.

In the previous age of insecurity, which lasted in Europe till after the end of the Napoleonic Wars, towns were defended by ring-walls, these walls were pierced by only a few gates, and these gates were closed at night. A traveller who arrived at a town gate after closing time had to wait outside the walls till the gate opened the next morning. One of my great-uncles (not the seaman) describes, in a journal that he kept, how in 1832, the year of Goethe's death, the diligence in which he was travelling from Aachen to Köln en route for the university of Bonn, had to hurry up in order to reach the west gate of Köln before this gate was closed for the night. Köln enclosed within walls pierced only by gates that were closed at nighttime! This is a picture of Köln that can hardly be imagined by anyone who knows the colossal sprawling, wall-less, gateless Köln of the present day.

An increasing use of clocks and watches in Western countries during the last six hundred years is evidence of an increasingly acute and meticulous time-consciousness. Till lately it has been taken for granted that this time-consciousness has come to stay, and that it will spread progressively, with the spread of the mechanized way of working, from the Western minority of mankind, among whom this novel way of working originally started, to the rest of the human race. This expectation is based on the assumption that urban factory work and office work is going to be a permanent and ubiquitous condition of human life. However, this assumption is now being called in question. It is being recognized that the Industrial Revolution carries within itself the seeds of its own demise. It has equipped mankind's perennial greed with such potent material means of self-indulgence that, if mankind does not now voluntarily restrain this innate greed, the eventual effect of the Industrial Revolution may be to exhaust mankind's irreplaceable natural resources and to make mankind's habitat uninhabitable by polluting it with poisonous waste products of mechanized industrial production.

If this forecast is correct, the now predominant way of life in the Western countries, in the Soviet Union, and in Japan may prove to be transient. Either voluntarily or involuntarily, it may be brought to an end, and the mechanized minority of mankind may have to revert to its previous way of life in which the staple means of livelihood was agriculture and animal husbandry. This is still the way in which a majority of the human race makes its living. It would be much more difficult to de-mechanize a community's way of life than it has been to mechanize it; and, if this is the destiny of the technologically "advanced" countries, these countries are going to have to pass through a period of very severe adversity in the near future. There may be no possibility of escaping from this. The natural resources provided for mankind by the planet that is our habitat are inexorably limited. It is conceivable that my great-grandchildren may have to try to live through an industrial counter-revolution. They will still be alive in the year 2050 if they live to my present age (I am now eighty-five).

In the year 2050, are clocks and watches going still to have the importance that they have in the year 1974? The thesis of this essay is that clocks and watches have been concomitants, instruments, and symbols of the mechanization of production and of the time-consciousness—the conciousness that "time is money"—which mechanization has brought with it. If this phase of human history proved to be as transitory as so many other phases that have preceded it, clocks and watches might become archaeological relics of a bygone age. They might be preserved as curiosities in museums, as sundials, spinning wheels, scythes, and instruments for grinding corn by hand are preserved in our museums today. However, in 1974, mechanization is not receding; so far from that, it is advancing with an increasing momentum. In the light of this, it seems probable to me that my great-grandchildren will be finding clocks and watches as indispensable for them as they are for me.

On clocks and their precursors,
on the inventors, makers and craftsmen
who made the passage of time
visible and measurable with these
"six hundred years of the world's most
beautiful timepieces"

Time is the ruler of all things
(Tempus rerum imperator)

Motto of the London Clockmakers' Guild

Table Clock of Philip the Good of Burgundy (first half of the 15th century)

Gilt bronze (height: 48 centimeters—19 inches)

Even though all questions about this clock have not been finally settled, it is properly at the beginning of this book, as the oldest extant clock with spring and fusee. A work of art of the very topmost rank.

Germanisches Nationalmuseum, Nuremberg

All the gold in the world
cannot retrieve one minute that is gone

Domenico Cavalca

In contrast to German Renaissance clocks, which were usually round or square, the early French clocks were often built on a polygonal plan, with the running and striking mechanisms arranged one over the other.

Astronomical Table Clock by Pierre de Fobis, Lyon (1535)
Gilt bronze (height: 17 centimeters–6¾ inches)

Dated and signed work from the early days of French clockmaking. A clock of very special importance.

Württembergisches Landesmuseum, Stuttgart (Fremersdorf Collection)

Table Clock by Nicolas Lemaindre, Blois (1619)
Brass and iron (height: 17 centimeters–6¾ inches)

This clock, originally mounted into a valuable case, was made for the French Queen Maria Medici. Her coat-of-arms and initials were worked into the openwork gears.

Private ownership

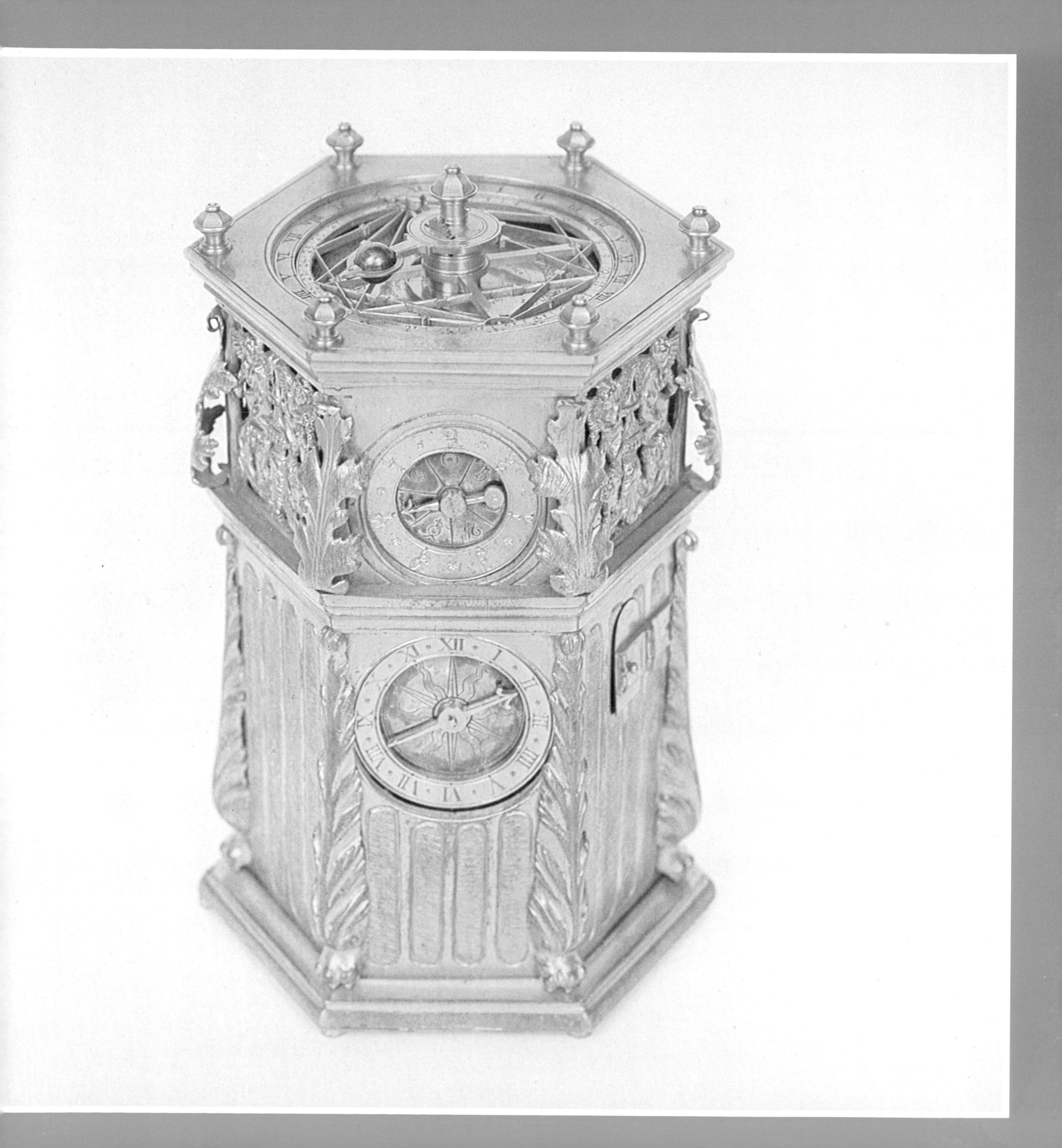

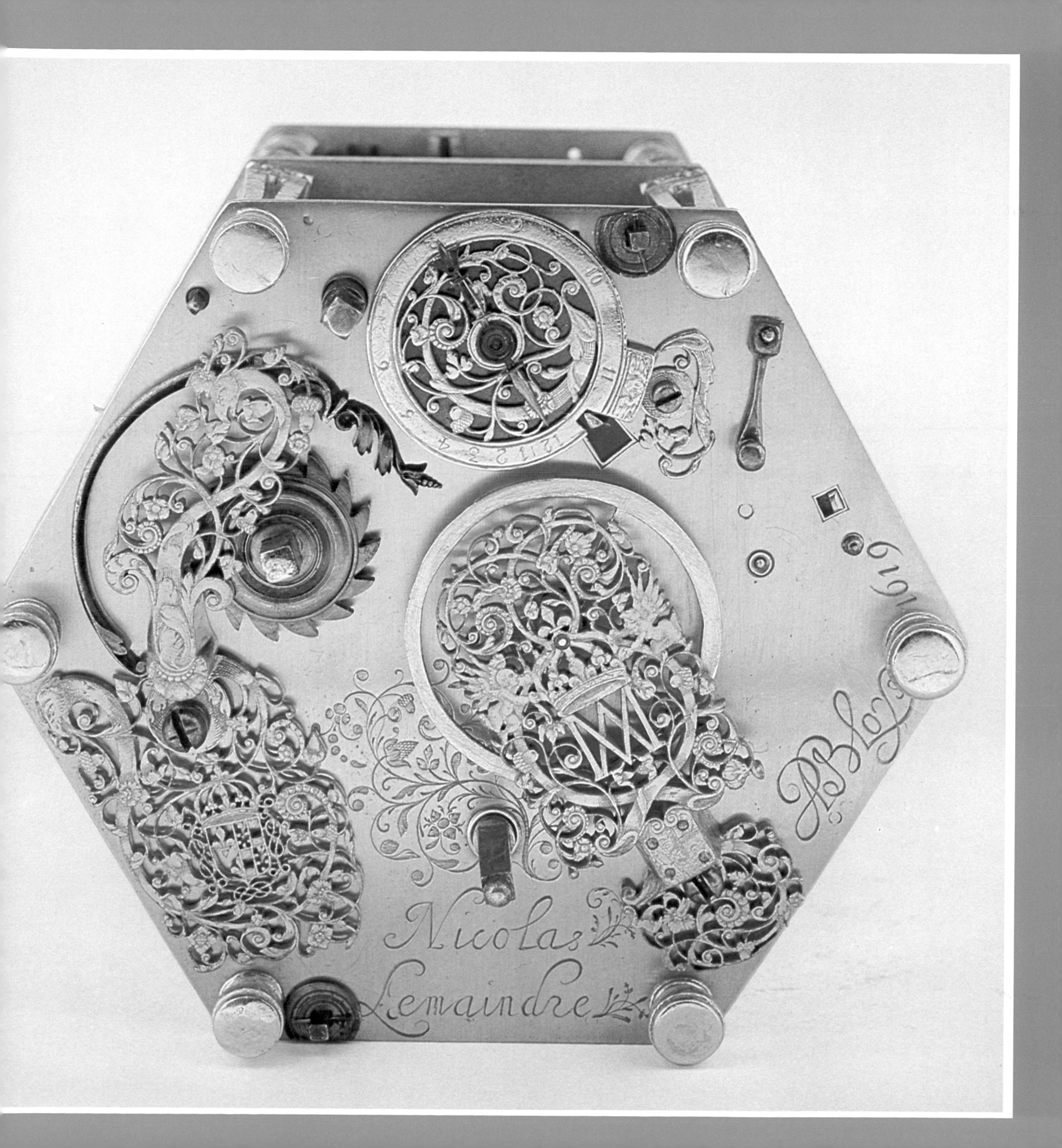
Nicolas
Lemaindre

I wasted time, and now doth time waste me;
For now hath time made me his numbering clock:
My thoughts are minutes; and with sighs they jar
Their watches on unto mine eyes, the outward watch,
Whereto my finger, like a dial's point
Is pointing still, in cleansing them from tears.
Now sir, the sound that tells what hour it is
Are clamorous groans, which strike upon my heart,
Which is the bell: so sighs and tears and groans
Show minutes, times, and hours...

William Shakespeare, King Richard II

"Emperor Monument Clock," Southern Germany (c. 1550)

Case ebony, jasper, and lapis lazuli; metal parts silver, gilt and partially enameled; works iron (height: 41 centimeters—16¼ inches)

This case, in the shape of a little temple, is unique among 16th-century clocks. The coat-of-arms and the seated emperor figure, attributed to Wenzel Jamnitzer, show that this clock was made for a ruler of the House of Hapsburg—probably Emperor Charles V or King Ferdinand I.

Württembergisches Landesmuseum, Stuttgart (Fremersdorf Collection)

Time is Man's angel

Friedrich Schiller, Wallenstein's Death

Among 16th-century table clocks, one group (nine clocks in all are known) is distinguished by the particularly rich decoration of its sides, on which the story of Orpheus and Eurydice is shown in deep relief: Orpheus, enchanting the many animals with his music, frees Eurydice from the Underworld.

Table Clock, Nuremberg (c. 1570)

Face embossed and gilt copper; case gilt bronze; works gilt brass (height: 7.6 centimeters—3 inches; diameter 23 centimeters—9⅛ inches)

The luxurious embossed work of the face is attributed to Wenzel Jamnitzer. The arrangement of the works, and the division of the face into six sections, suggest an Italian client.

Württembergisches Landesmuseum, Stuttgart (Fremersdorf Collection)

Table Clock, Nuremberg (c. 1570)

Gilt bronze; works iron (height: 9 centimeters—3⅝ inches; diameter 21 centimeters—8⅜ inches)

The most unusual of the "Orpheus Clocks"; the oldest known clock with a second hand. Besides hours, minutes, and seconds, the richly ornamented face shows the sun's position in the zodiac, day and date, and engraved pictures of the moon (after Virgil Solis).

Württembergisches Landesmuseum, Stuttgart (Fremersdorf Collection)

DIES IOVIS
IVNIVS
MAIVS
IVLIVS
DIES VENERIS
APRILIS
AVGVSTVS
MARTIVS
SEPTEMBER
FEBRVARIVS
OCTOBER
IANVARIVS
NOVEMBER
DECEMBER
DIES LVNAE

Who presses time will find himself pressed by time

Old saying

"Ostrich with Bear Cub," Automaton Clock, Nuremberg? (c. 1580)

Case gilt copper; works iron (height: 50 centimeters—19¾ inches)

When the quarter hour strikes, the bear opens its mouth and moves its head. On the hour, the bird moves its beak, rolls its eyes, and flaps its wings. When the alarm is released, the bear beats the drum. It may be identical to an ostrich acquired by Archduke Ferdinand in Augsburg in 1584.

Württembergisches Landesmuseum, Stuttgart (Fremersdorf Collection)

Ship Automaton, perhaps by Hanns Schlott, Prague (c. 1580)

Gilt copper (height: 100 centimeters—39⅜ inches)

A real toy for adults, this table automaton is in the shape of a ship that rolls across the table. It was probably made for Emperor Rudolf II. The sailors in the crow's nests strike the hours on bells, organ music sounds, and the Electors, along with many other moving figures, strut around the Emperor's throne.

British Museum, London

"Topsy-Turvy World," Centerpiece, Augsburg (c. 1580)

Wood and gilt bronze (height: 92 centimeters—36¼ inches)

Above the moving monkey circled by the group of hunters, a second smaller row of figures of forest animals moves on a central structure supported by eight slender round columns.

Mathematisch-Physikalischer Salon, Dresden

Time is often said to be money, but it is more—
it is life

Avebury, Pleasures of Life

Necklace Watch, marked and dated "CS 1562"

Silver, gilt brass, and iron

Miniature table clocks are actually the early "Nürnberger Ührlein"—"Little Nuremberg Watches" —an appellation which, through a misunderstanding, became the later "Nürnberger Eierlein" —"Little Nuremberg Eggs." In drum-shaped cases, worn at the neck and often richly ornamented and fitted with simple works, they are the forerunners of the pocket watch. These wearable watches were made possible by the new "stackfreed"—an arrangement to equalize slackening spring tension. Its invention is attributed to Peter Henlein, who thus should have earned the reputation of "inventor" of the pocket watch.

Museo Poldi Pezzoli, Milan

Time is but an empty room, to which only events, thoughts, and feelings give content

Wilhelm von Humboldt, Letters

The most usual type of 16th-century table clock was quadrangular, either square or oblong, with faces on the front and back. Many indicators, and luxurious decoration, are characteristic of these showpieces, generally destined for the collections and treasure chambers of princely persons.

Table Clock by Jeremias Metzger, Augsburg (1564)

Gilt bronze; works iron (height: 29.7 centimeters—11¾ inches)

The case, richly decorated with figures, the free and still asymmetrical arrangement of the faces, and the high quality of the workmanship make this clock the most important example of its type from the mid-16th century.

Kunsthistorisches Museum, Vienna

Threefold is the step of time:
Hesitant, the Future draws anon,
An arrow swift is Now a-gone,
And the Past eternally stands firm

Friedrich Schiller, Sayings of Confucius

The large astronomical clocks in which celestial events—in accordance with the development of the science up to that time—could be mechanically reproduced are high points of 16th-century watchmaking and of precision mechanics in general.

Planet Clock by Eberhard Baldewein and Hans Bucher, Dresden (1563–1567)

(height: 135 centimeters—53¼ inches)

The planetary orbits, showing the movements around the sun of Mars, Venus, Mercury, Saturn, and Jupiter according to the Ptolemaic world-picture, are arranged on the four viewing sides. On the lower half of the pictured side is the astrolabe, operated by the clockworks, and above this the orbit of the planet Mars. The rear side shows a perpetual calendar and the movements of the moon. The following pages show details of this clock.

Mathematisch-Physikalischer Salon, Dresden

XII
XI
X
IX
VIII
VII
VI
V
IIII
III
II
I
DECEMBER
NOVEMBER
IANVARIVS
FEBRVARIVS
MARTIVS
PRILIS
MAIVS
IVNIVS
IVLIVS
AVGVSTVS
SEPTEMBER
OCTOBER
CAN. MAIOR
LVCIDA HYDRÆ
GEMINI
CANCE
LEO
VIRGO
LIBRA
CORPIVS
SAGITTARI
CAPRICORN
AQVARIVS
PISCES
ARIES
SPICA
CORONA
AQVILA
MVSC.
PEGASI
CAP. SERPEN.
CAP. HERC.
CAVDA
MIRACH
NARIS CETI
SIN. PES ORI.
DEX. HVME. ORI.
CAVDA CETI

ELEVA POLI

Time Works Wonders

Douglas Jerrold, Play title

Wood-Cased Clock by Hans Kiening, Füssen (1577–1578)

Wood and paper, painted; brass, zinc, and iron (height: 100 centimeters—39⅜ inches)

Simple in its outer appearance and in material, and therefore all the richer in its ample horological and astronomical information (it even shows the appropriate Sabbath Gospel reading for each Sunday), this weighted clock is actually a reduced monumental clock, such as were mounted in churches, and primarily in city halls, in the 16th century.

Kunsthistorisches Museum, Vienna

Wall Clock, Saxony? (second half of the 16th century)

Iron, gilt bronze (height: 44 centimeters—17⅜ inches)

Judging from the coat-of-arms, this clock was made for an Elector of Saxony. The side panels are painted with Turkish horsemen, and the gilt front shows the face divided into hours and minutes.

Württembergisches Landesmuseum, Stuttgart (Fremersdorf Collection)

House Clock, probably Strasbourg (second half of the 16th century)

Painted iron (height: 40 centimeters—15⅞ inches)

Simple in materials and appearance, this clock is remarkable for its abundance of indicators and for the rich painting. On the side is a picture of the clockmaker or owner winding this clock.

Württembergisches Landesmuseum, Stuttgart (Fremersdorf Collection)

An disem Astronomischen Instrument ist ein Ewigwerender Kalender mit den für-
ANO DNI MILE QVIN SEPTVA OCTAVO
MENSES SIGNORVM DESCENDENTIVM
MENSES SIGNORVM ASCENDENTIVM
IOANES PINICIANVS PICTORMEFFECI

We seek to banish time,
and at last it does us the favor
of allowing itself to be banished;
finally it leaves us altogether.
Then Eternity is here.

Werner Bergengruen

Globe Clock by Johannes Reinhold and Georg Roll, Augsburg (1584)
Gilt, ebony (height: 80 centimeters—31⅝ inches)

The works of this clock are in the large celestial globe, which revolves once every 24 hours and allows many astronomical observations. In the base are four sundials, in the stand an earth globe, and on top there is a small armillary sphere.

Mathematisch-Physikalischer Salon, Dresden

Time wasted is existence, us'd is life

Edward Young

Table Automaton by Paulus Schuster, Nuremberg (1585)
(height: 80 centimeters—31⅝ inches)

Similar in outward appearance to the tower-shaped table clocks, this automaton, almost a yard tall, has numerous figures—moving monkeys and revolving hunt and animal groups—and a richly decorated base, in which the works are located.

Mathematisch-Physikalischer Salon, Dresden

Table Clock by Hans Gruber, Nuremberg (1583)
Silver, bronze, and gilt copper (height: 37 centimeters—14⅝ inches)

Besides the extraordinarily rich relief decoration, the plethora of indicators is the chief attraction of this particularly precious table clock.

Württembergisches Landesmuseum, Stuttgart

Table Clock, enamel decoration by David Attemstetter, Augsburg (c. 1600)
Silver, partially gilt, enameled (height: 21.8 centimeters—8⅝ inches)

Of the same type as Metzger's clock but more precious in materials, brilliantly colorful and of a timeless, well-balanced beauty, this clock shows, on the rear side pictured here, the hours, the sun's position in the zodiac, and the lunar date. On the front: hours and minutes, day of the week, and phase of the sun.

Kunsthistorisches Museum, Vienna

MÆSTA TRAHIT TARDAM
SORTE GRAVANTE MORAM

Time has sharp teeth

Norwegian saying

The early wearable watches were also jewelry. They were not carried in the pocket, but rather worn on a cord or chain on the chest, and appear in many different forms: round, rectangular, or oval, or in the shape of a heart, cross, or star. They are always richly adorned and decorated.

Star-Shaped Necklace Watch by David Ramsay, London (c. 1600)

Ramsay was a Scot, the Court Clockmaker to King James VI of Scotland. The richly engraved case, however, is not his, but is signed "De Heck sculp."

Clockmakers Company, London

Cross Watch by Conrad Kreizer, Strasbourg (c. 1600)

Gold enamel and rock crystal (height: 8.8 centimeters–3 inches)

Decorated with colored enamel, and sheltering in a crystal case, this cross watch combines magnificence with piety, and love of decoration with thoughts of transitoriness.

Private ownership

Necklace Watch (c. 1625)

Gold, enamel, rock crystal, and pearls

Magnificent oval necklace watch with one hand, the cover cut in facets, and side panels of rock crystal with pearl trim and delicate wrought gold.

Mathematisch-Physikalischer Salon, Dresden

I shall not scold you, wondrous hour,
That you have gone so quickly past:
You brought to me the sweet good news
My heart is not yet dead, outcast

Friedrich Hebbel

Mantel Clock by Michael Sneeberger, Prague (1606)

Gold and semiprecious stones (height: 12.6 centimeters—5 inches)

The works of this clock are of particularly painstakingly worked gilt brass, because they are housed in a rock crystal case and visible from all sides. The drum is decorated with garnets, and below its hinged lid is a horizontal clockface, on which hours, minutes, and lunar date are shown.

Kunsthistorisches Museum, Vienna

Time which is the author of all authors

Francis Bacon, Essays: "Of the Advancement of Learning"

Besides the representative clocks built as large as possible, there were, as early as the 16th and 17th centuries, very small and delicate watches, made as small as possible and richly and preciously decorated—masterpieces of the art of the goldsmiths as well as that of the clockmakers.

Table Clock by Andreas Rabe, Hamburg (1638)

Silver, partially gilt, rock crystal (height: 37 centimeters—14⅝ inches)

This eight-sided clock with its magnificent putto is a valuable witness to northern German handicrafts of the 17th century. It shows the hours and quarter hours, day, date, and phase of the moon.

Museo Poldi Pezzoli, Milan

Small Table Clock, Southern Germany (1596)

Silver and gilt bronze (height: 18 centimeters—7⅛ inches)

The works of a necklace watch, probably French, were placed in a three-sided case decorated with an enameled coat-of-arms and mounted on a delicate stand. The arms indicate the probable giver or recipient as Duke Friedrich of Württemberg.

Württembergisches Landesmuseum, Stuttgart

Table Clock, Prague (c. 1600–1610)

Gilt silver, semiprecious stones (height: 21 centimeters—8⅜ inches)

In this clock, too, necklace watches were used and mounted on a stand of turned agate. A product of the Imperial Court Workshop in Prague.

Kunsthistorisches Museum, Vienna

Mars
Mercuri
Sol

A dream is but our life, a dream
Here on the earth;
As shadows on the billows do
We float and fade
And measure off our sluggish steps
By space and time;
And are (and know not) at the core
Of the eterne

Johann Gottfried Herder

Folding Sundial by Hans Tucher, Nuremberg (first quarter of the 17th century)
Ivory and gilt bronze (11 × 7 centimeters—4⅜ × 2¾ inches)

Ivory sundials, also known simply as "compasses" because of the compass needle placed on them, were an important export article for Nuremberg as early as the 15th century. They generally combine a vertical clock with a horizontal one, and allow the reading of zodiac and lunar time.

Württembergisches Landesmuseum, Stuttgart

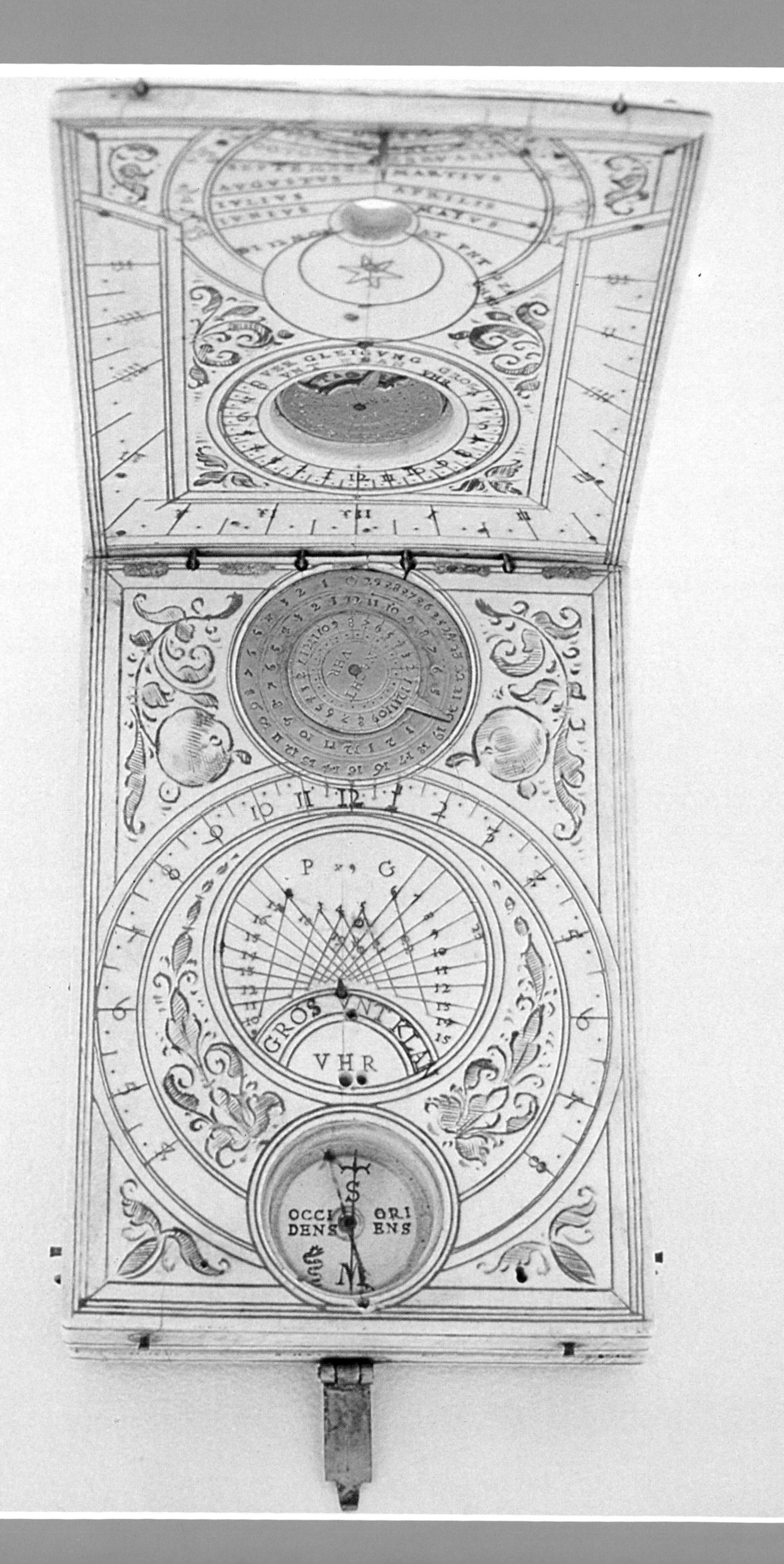
AVGVSTVS
MARTIVS
IVLIVS
APRILIS
IVNIVS
MAIVS
P
G
GROS VNT KLAIN
VHR
S
OCCI
DENS
ORI
ENS
N

Patience, reason, and time
Make possible the impossible

Friedrich Rückert

Automatic accessory figurines were often more important than exact time indicators. These automatons were showpieces in princely art chambers, and most were made in Nuremberg or Augsburg.

"Diana on the Centaur," Automaton Clock, Augsburg (c. 1600)
Silver, partially gilt, fitted with gems and enameled; base ebony (height: 39.5 centimeters—15⅝ inches)

The automaton rolls across the table, the centaur moves his eyes and shoots, Diana and the dogs move their heads.

Kunsthistorisches Museum, Vienna

"Lion," Automaton Clock, Augsburg (c. 1600)
Ebony, silver, and gilt bronze (height: 23 centimeters—9⅛ inches)

The lion's eyes move back and forth with the balance, so the running of the clock can be seen. When the hour strikes, the lion's mouth moves.

Württembergisches Landesmuseum, Stuttgart

"Parrot," Automaton Clock, Augsburg (c. 1600)
Base ebony; bird gilt copper (height: 40 centimeters—15⅞ inches)

This bird whistles the hours with a pair of mechanically moved bellows, simultaneously moving his beak, wings, and eyes; at the same time his hind end drops as many balls as the number of hours.

Bayerisches Nationalmuseum, Munich

2721.

Time, a flaming giantess, strides calmly on,
not caring about the yelping
of biting clerics and aristocrats below

Heinrich Heine, Travel Pictures

Necklace Watch, Nuremberg (second half of the 16th century)

Gilt bronze

A richly engraved one-handed watch, worn at the neck on a chain or cord as jewelry; its openwork lid permitted reading of the time even when closed.

Abeler Collection, Wuppertal

Coach Clock by Pierre Roux, Blois (c. 1635)

Larger portable clocks were, depending on their destination, called travel clocks, coach clocks, or saddle clocks. The present example from Blois, the main French clockmaking city in the 17th century, has an alarm and a striking mechanism to tell the hours.

Private collection

Oval Necklace Watch, France (c. 1620)

Along with the simple one-handed movement, this richly engraved French watch also has an alarm arrangement: The inner disk was turned so that the hand showed the desired hour at its edge.

Private collection

Time is money—says the vulgarest saw known to any age or people. Turn it round about, and you get a precious truth—money is time.

George Gissing, The Private Papers of Henry Ryecroft: "Winter"

The 17th century was a time of revolution and experimentation in clockmaking. Artisans aspired to new case shapes, longer running time, constant drive, and greater exactitude; and cross-beat escapement and the rolling-ball clock were tested along with balance and axle drive. These efforts culminated successfully in the introduction of the pendulum by Huygens.

Tower-Shaped Table Clock by J. Sayller, Ulm (c. 1630)

Case silver, partially gilt; works iron and brass (height: 57 centimeters—22½ inches)

Two things distinguish this clock—the massive silver case, and the works, which run for about a quarter of a year when a constant drive is applied. Each time the striking mechanism, with its huge spring and fusee, is released, it winds up the smaller spring of the drive mechanism just a bit, so its tension is always constant.

Württembergisches Landesmuseum, Stuttgart

Time Waits Only for the Devil

Popular song title

Table Clock by David Buschmann, Augsburg (second half of the 17th century)
Wood, gilt brass, silver partially enameled (height: 69.5 centimeters—27½ inches)

Made after the pattern of an invention by the elder Buschmann, this clock's hand springs back at the end of a semicircular scale; it is linked with a sundial, so that the precision of the geared clock can be checked.

Kunsthistorisches Museum, Vienna

Table Clock by Nikolaus Planckh, Augsburg (mid-17th century)
Bronze, copper, and gilt brass (height: 81 centimeters—32 inches)

Because of their similarity with monstrances, clocks of this type are, somewhat unfortunately, called monstrance clocks. They usually have a great many indicators. This clock, for example, shows—besides minutes and the various types of hours—an astrolabe and calendarium on its front. On the rear side: regulating clockfaces, day of the week, and the position of the sun in the zodiac.

Kunsthistorisches Museum, Vienna

Figurine Clock by Johannes Buschmann, Augsburg (c. 1624)
Ebony, silver, partially gilt (height: 74.5 centimeters—29⅜ inches)

The religious-allegorical accessory works are the main attraction of this clock: A "Little Death," carved of ivory by the Munich craftsman Christoph Angermeir, turns—moved by the clockworks—as a reminder of the death of all things.

Kunsthistorisches Museum, Vienna

Pillar-Shaped Table Clock by David Buschmann, Augsburg (second half of the 17 century)
Silver and bronze, partially gilt, tortoiseshell, and wood (height: 75 centimeters—29⅝ inches)

This clock was shaped in the form of a monument—like, for example, the Mary Pillar in Munich. The hours are marked by a hand sliding downward in a spiral.

Kunsthistorisches Museum, Vienna

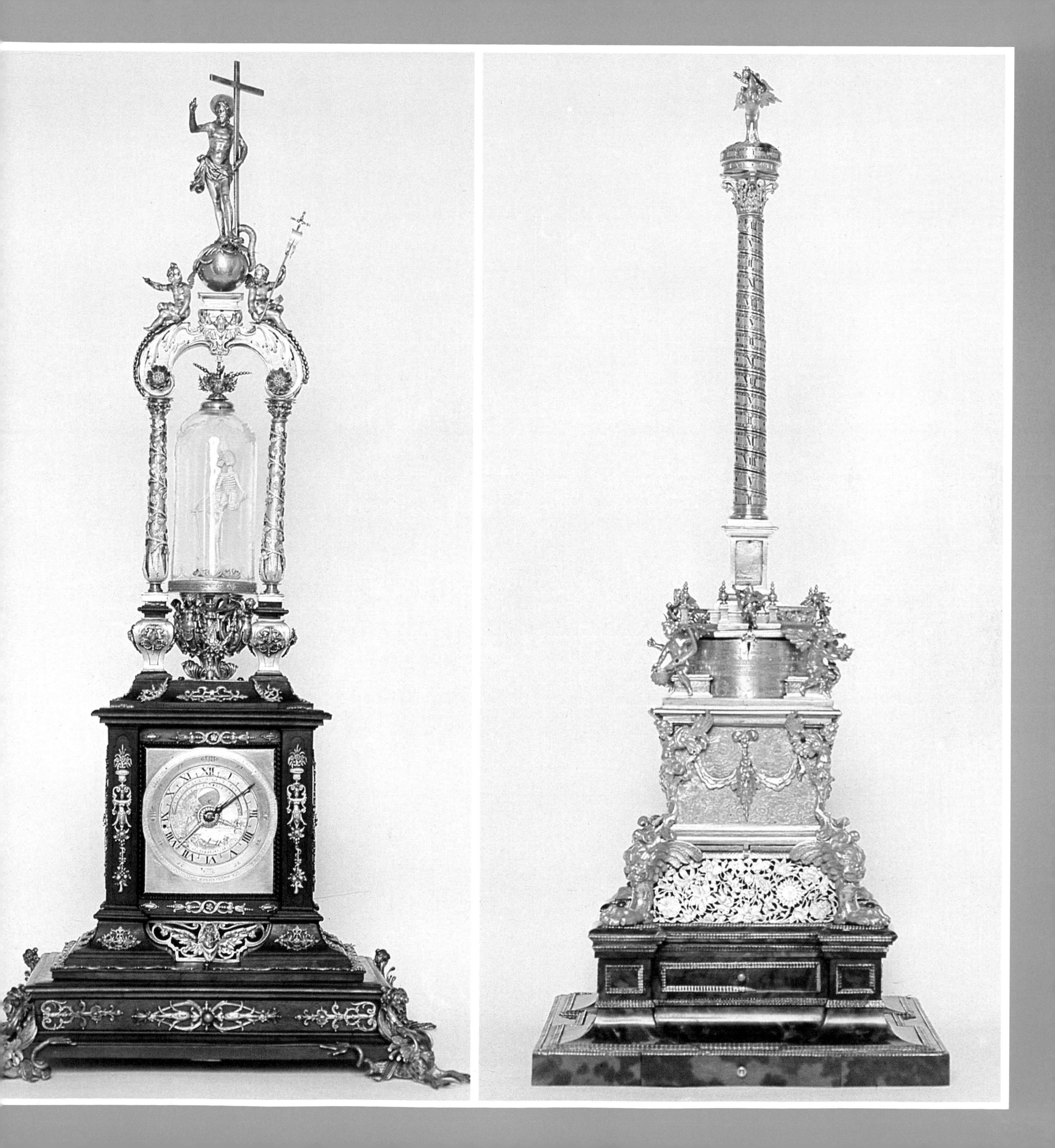

Of course, I think watches are superfluous.
You see, I live very near City Hall. Every morning when I go to work,
I look up at the City Hall clock to see what time it is,
and I memorize it for the whole day; that way I don't
wear out my watch quite as much

Karl Valentin

Necklace Watch by Jean Rousseau, Orléans (c. 1650)

In the shape of a tulip blossom, the glass on three sides permits an unhindered view of the face and works of this necklace watch.

Private ownership

Time is the greatest innovator

Francis Bacon, Essays: "Of Innovations"

Necklace Watch by Estienne Hubert, Rouen (c. 1620–1630)

Gilt brass, carnelians

The principal charm of this exceptional, preciously worked piece lies in the deep color of the carnelian, of which both the front and rear lids are worked.

Museo Poldi Pezzoli, Milan

Necklace Watch, Southern Germany (c. 1650)

Gilt brass, rock crystal

The shell-shaped lid of this ingeniously worked decorative watch, unusual in its outline, permits a view of the works. The striking mechanism bell, therefore, was hidden between the works and the face.

Museo Poldi Pezzoli, Milan

At the beginning of the 17th century, decorating clockfaces and cases with colored enamel painting became common in France. Besides trimming with gems and embossing, enamel remained until modern times the most successful material with which timepieces were changed into jewelry pieces.

Necklace Watch by David Bouquet, London (mid-17th century)

Silver, gilt brass, enamel

This magnificent English necklace watch is covered inside and out with mythological scenes painted in enamel. The inner side, pictured, shows Narcissus at the spring.

Museo Poldi Pezzoli, Milan

Enamel Watch, Works by Jeremias Flug, Passau (c. 1665); case, Blois

Silver, gold, turquoise, and enamel

The outside of this watch is trimmed with turquoises; inside, all the surfaces are decorated with cameo-colored paintings—on the face a landscape, on the inside of the lid Adonis parting from Venus.

Wilsdorf Collection, Rolex, Geneva

Knowst what in this world it be,
That thing that does best please me?
That Time doth consume itself—
The world shall not forever be

Friedrich von Logau

Necklace Watch by Jean de Choudens, Rouen (c. 1670)
Enameled gold

Rectangular watches were a short-lived fad around 1670. Liselotte von der Pfalz sent such a watch to the Elector of Hannover; it was delayed at the post office, and she was afraid it would be out of fashion by the time it arrived. In the pictured watch, the hand is an enameled Amor, telling the time with the point of his arrow.

Museo Poldi Pezzoli, Milan

Necklace Watch by Joseph Norris Anglois, Amsterdam (c. 1680); enamel signed "Huaud le Puisné"
Gold, enamel

The Brothers Huaud were the most highly regarded enamelers of their time; they worked mostly on watch-decorating. The rear side of this watch shows the "Caritas Romana"—"Roman Charity"—the Athenian woman who nurses her father, who is wasting away in prison, with her own milk.

Museo Poldi Pezzoli, Milan

Necklace Watch, France (second half of the 17th century); enamel signed "Frères Huaud"

While the case of this watch, with its beautiful enamel painting by the Brothers Huaud, was kept, the works were later replaced by a Nuremberg clockmaker.

Musée des Arts Décoratifs, Paris

That minute weighs heavy
which slips away and of which one does not know
whether it will end,
no matter how much time one has to observe it

Eugène Guillevic

Pocket Watch by M. Marcou, Amsterdam (c. 1700)

The middle hand tells the minutes, while by day a little sun, by night a moon, show the hours through a cutout. The date in the cutout below and the little automaton bespeak the interest of the era in technical peculiarities.

Musée des Arts Décoratifs, Paris

60
5
10
15
20
25
30
35
40
45
50
55
21

It happens in an hour that comes not in an age

Thomas Fuller, Gnomologia

Show Clock by Joseph Anton Schoener, Augsburg (c. 1700)

Wood and tortoiseshell, silver, brass, and iron (height: 120 centimeters—47⅜ inches)

Built up like an altar clock with rich indicators, the works of this clock remain those of a traditional tower-shaped table clock. It has a second viewing side with astrolabe and numerous auxiliary faces.

Württembergisches Landesmuseum, Stuttgart

Monstrance Clock, Augsburg (second half of the 17th century)

Wood, gilt bronze, silver (height: 50 centimeters—19¾ inches)

A Negro supports the clock with its bizarrely shaped background, which is richly decorated with silver embossing—perhaps by Balthasar Gelb. The clock itself is actually a coach clock, later rebuilt to accommodate pendulum movement.

Württembergisches Landesmuseum, Stuttgart

In the second half of the 17th century, Augsburg produced clocks which are remarkable for their rich embossed-silver ornamentation. J. A. Thelot was the leading master, and most clocks of this type are ascribed to him or his workshop.

Plate Clock by Hans Otto Halleicher, Augsburg (c. 1680); silver embossing probably by J. A. Thelot

Silver, brass, and iron (height: 45.5 centimeters—18 inches)

Chronos, the god of time, points with his staff to the hours on the revolving disk. Around it is the entire ancient mythological heaven, with numerous allegorical figures.

Württembergisches Landesmuseum, Stuttgart

Time, it is a blooming field,
And nature a great living one,
And all is fruit and all is seed

Friedrich Schiller, The Bride of Messina

Besides decorative watches, timepieces with unusually rich indicators and strangely carved faces are characteristic of wearable watches of the 17th century.

Necklace Watch for the Turkish Market (17th century)

Silver and niello

In the 17th century European clockmakers, and natives working under their supervision, made timepieces that matched contemporary European clocks in their works while being suited to Oriental taste in case decoration, in script, and in ornamentation. The inside of the lid is ornamented with niello, the face shows hour, day and date, phase of the moon, and lunar time.

Omega Collection, Biel, Switzerland

Immeasurably long Time begets everything
from its dark womb
and hides again that which appears

Sophocles, Ajax

"Night Clock" by Petrus Thomas Campanus, Rome (1683)

Ebony, oak, gilt brass, marble, lapis lazuli (height: 100 centimeters—39⅜ inches)

An Italian specialty, especially in the 17th century, was the night clock. Instead of a hand, the hour numbers move in a cutout arc past the quarter-hour indicators. Because the numbers are of openwork, the clock can also be read at night if there is a lamp behind it.

British Museum, London

Monstrance Clock by Thomas Starck, South Germany (1620); case, French (c. 1680)

(height: 75 centimeters—29¼ inches)

An exceedingly happy "marriage" (as combining clocks of different origins is called) is this combination of a German monstrance clock of the early 17th century with the case of a French tortoiseshell clock of the late 17th century, both of them of the highest quality. On the unusually beautiful rear side, six silver and enamel faces show all the information that could be expected from an astronomical clock of this period. On the front side are an astrolabe and indicators of day and night.

British Museum, London

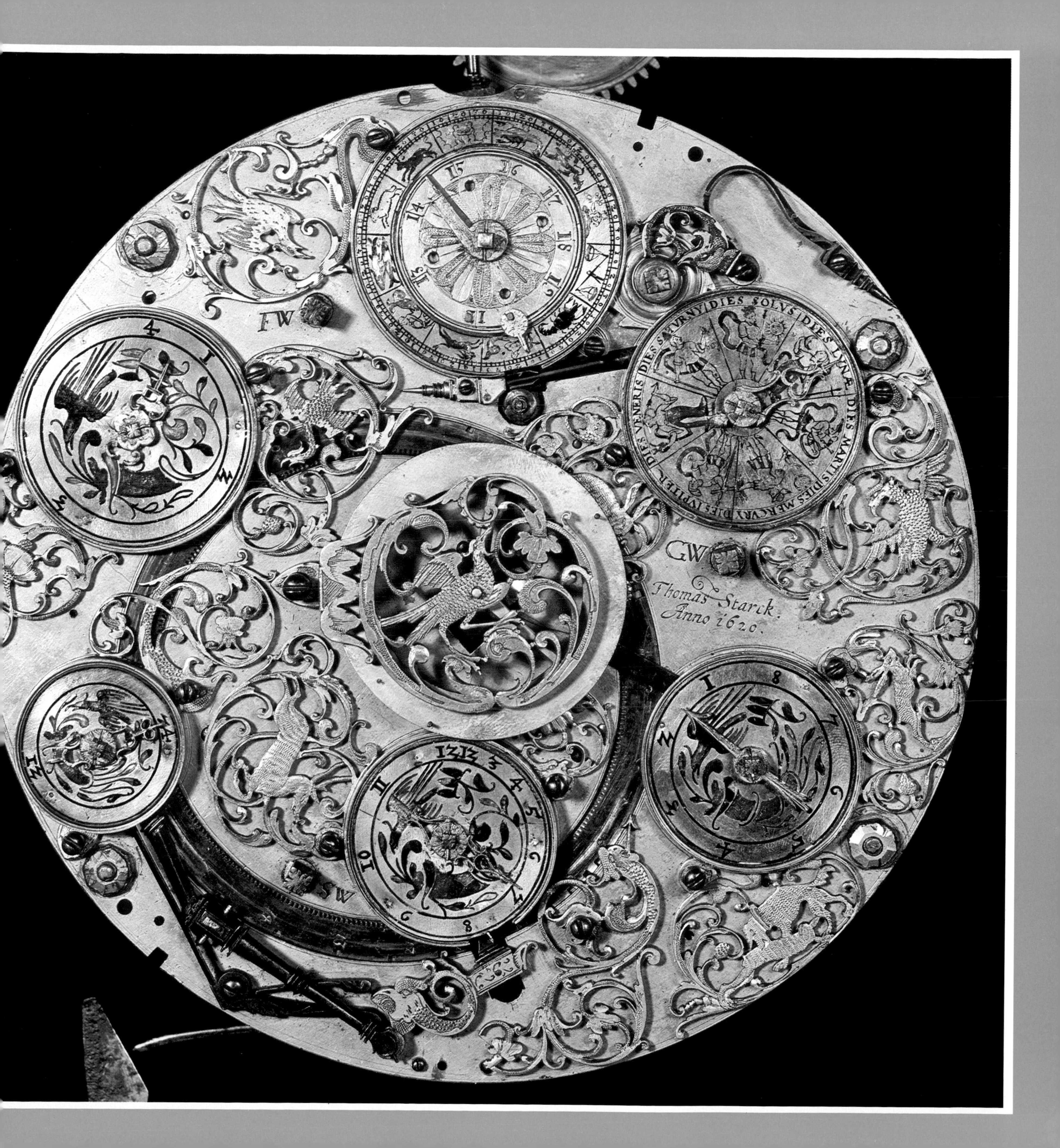
FW
DIES SATVRNY DIES SOLVS DIES LVNÆ
DIES MARTIS DIES MERCVRY DIES IVPITER DIES VENERIS
GW
Thomas Starck
Anno 1620
SW

It is an old and a true saying, that
"An hour in the morning before breakfast
is worth two all the rest of the day"

William Hone, Every-Day Book

Long-Case Clock by Jacques Thuret, Paris (c. 1700); case attributed to A. C. Boulle
Oak, tortoiseshell, gilt bronze (height: 220 centimeters—86¾ inches)

In this particularly sumptuous floor clock, the origin of its shape is still clearly visible. It is a clock, very similar to the table or bureau clocks, placed on a pedestal for the security of the pendulum.

The Metropolitan Museum of Art, New York (Rogers Fund, 1958)

The right time decides everything—
At once it is victorious

Sophocles

Astronomical-Geographical Art Clock by Johann Klein, Prague (1738)

This clock is valuable on its outside too, but what is special about it is the Jesuit Father Sichelbarth's earth globe, built into the clockface; it is enameled, and is moved by the works. It makes possible many geographical and astronomical observations.

Mathematisch-Physikalischer Salon, Dresden

Mantel Clock by William Holloway, London (beginning of the 18th century)

Wood, silver, and gilt brass (height: 40 centimeters—15⅞ inches)

Beside the normally monochromatic English clock cases of this time, this "Bracket Clock" is noticeable for its painting of columbines, roses, carnations, and narcissi. The works have an ornamented pendulum, visible from the front, to check the movement.

Württembergisches Landesmuseum, Stuttgart

Pendulum Clock by Pierre Gaudron, Paris (c. 1700)

Wood decorated in Boulle technique (height: 50 centimeters—19¾ inches)

The sun, moving up and down in the slit of the revolving disk, shows the hour and sunrise and sunset times; the hand from the center shows the minutes; the lower face the moon phase and lunar date. The clock is an early and rare example of the use of the pendulum with cord suspension and cycloidal cheeks.

Abeler Collection, Wuppertal

William Holloway
London
Strike
Silent
16

GAUDRON A PARIS

Centuries pass quickly;
it is the years and hours that take time

Werner Bergengruen

World Time Clock by Andreas Gärtner, Dresden (c. 1730)

The large disk with 360 small faces moves once around its axis every 24 hours, together with the hand. The faces—matching 360 longitudinal lines—are attached at one-degree intervals, and have short hands that swing downward, showing the time everywhere in the world in comparison to Dresden.

Mathematisch-Physikalischer Salon, Dresden

Hourglasses remind us not only of the swift passage of time, but at the same time of the dust into which we will one day decay

Georg Christoph Lichtenberg

Pulpit Hourglass, Southern Germany (c. 1750)

Copper and gilt bronze (height: 37 centimeters—14⅝ inches)

Even now, the hourglass remains in use for measuring short time spans. In the 18th century it was particularly popular as a pulpit clock: It showed the cleric how long he must—or could—continue to preach.

Württembergisches Landesmuseum, Stuttgart

The best-used time is that which is lost

Claude Tellier, quoted by Austin Dobson, A Dialogue from Plato

Multifaceted Sundial, Southern Germany (18th century)

Alabaster (height: 14 centimeters—5½ inches)

Hour lines are engraved on all the flat and concave surfaces; the shadow of an edge shows the time along these lines according to the position of the sun. Usually made of stone, such clocks were preferred especially in parks and pleasure grounds.

Württembergisches Landesmuseum, Stuttgart

Equatorial Sundials by J. G. Zimmer, Reinharz Castle (c. 1750)

Magnificent pieces from the studio of Imperial Count Löser. To set correctly, the minute face must be turned until the gnomon's shadow falls on the mark line. These clockfaces connect to the hour faces by a cogwheel arrangement, enabling the viewer to read the exact time in minutes and hours.

Mathematisch-Physikalischer Salon, Dresden

Polyhedral Sundial by Hans Koch, Esslingen (1578)

Brass, gilt and enameled (height: 26 centimeters—10¼ inches)

Called "Polyedrum horodictium," this universal sundial was intended for Duke Ludwig of Württemberg. There are faces engraved on 25 surfaces, permitting reading at every time of year and day.

Bayerisches Nationalmuseum, Munich

MERIDIES
ORIENS

ELEVATIO POLI
SEPTENTRIO
HORIZONT
VIGILATE QVIA NE
SCITIS QVA HORA DO
MINVS VESTER VE
NTVRVS SIT
Mat: 24

Time is sure a wonderworking god.
In but one hour do run
Many thousand grains of sand;
Just as fast as these
Do move the thoughts of man

Friedrich Schiller, Wallenstein's Death

Wall Clock by Charles Cressent; works by Jean Godde l'Ainé, France (c. 1730)
Gilt bronze (height: 133 centimeters—52 1/2 inches)

This type of wall clock originated in the blending of clock and console, with richly moving contours and luxuriant figured decoration in gilt bronze. Above, cherub with hourglass; below, winged Chronos with his scythe.

The Metropolitan Museum of Art, New York (Collection of Mr. and Mrs. Charles B. Wrightsman)

Time is the best medicine

Netherlands saying

Pendulum Clock on Console by Louis Panier, Paris (c. 1743)
Wood, gilt bronze, and enamel

Pendulum clocks of this sort were made in great numbers in the first half of the 18th century in Paris, and—richly decorated with gilt bronze—were ornamented in the most diverse techniques: painted and lacquered, covered with colored tortoiseshell, inlaid in Boulle technique.

Private ownership

Console Clock with Musical Automaton by Andreas Lehner, Munich (first half of the 18th century)
Wood, brass, gilt bronze, and iron (total height: 197 centimeters—77½ inches)

A set of chimes, with three melodies on eleven bells, is built in between the stand and the clock. The pendulum is a swing with a comedy figure.

Württembergisches Landesmuseum, Stuttgart

Pendulum Clock by Alexandre le Bon, Paris (first third of the 18th century)

Deriving from a Boulle design—which was, however, meant for a console clock— this timepiece is an example of how a console or mantel clock set in a base becomes its own type: the long-case clock.

Louvre, Paris

Long-Case Clock by Jean Chorot, Paris (1745–1748); case and bronzes by Jean Pierre Latz
Gilt silver, bronze, and various woods (height: 226 centimeters—89 inches)

Aside from the magnificent case, the complicated works above all are remarkable. They show the time equation—the difference between true sun time and median local time— and contain a perpetual calendar which even takes leap years into account. Date, day, lunar date, and sunrise and sunset times in hours and minutes are shown. One of the most important clocks of the midcentury.

Württembergisches Landesmuseum, Stuttgart

Use time well by day and night
And always earnestly be 'ware
That youth shall quickly pass us by
Just like a flower or the air

Old saying

Philipp Matthaeus Hahn (1739–1790) is probably the most important layperson among the many hobbyists who were interested in clockmaking. A country parson, he busied himself with mathematics, astronomy, and the technical problems of complex astronomical machines, pocket watches, sundials, and scales, which were made following his instructions by traveling artisans and some permanent collaborators.

Astronomical Clock by P. M. Hahn, Kornwestheim (1780)

Simple in its outward shape but equipped with many astronomical indicators, this clock shows a Copernican system—the movement of the earth with the moon around the sun—as well as a geocentric system with the apparent movements of sun, moon, and Venus.

Württembergisches Landesmuseum, Stuttgart

Philipp Matth. Hahn

The sun, which from itself births time and cleaves it,
Will pass on with time, which hastens to its goal.
Yet he is beyond the time and sun, and lives and lives,
On whom the Lord doth shine, the sun that never sets

Andreas Gryphius

Mantel Clock, marked "Ridel a Paris" (c. 1800)

Gilt bronze, enamel (height: 53.5 centimeters—21⅛ inches)

Elegant in shape, grand and precious in its combination of gilt bronze, pale marble, and colored enamel, this clock is remarkable particularly for its rich indicators (interest in such things began to recur in the last half of the 18th century). It has a second hand, date and day indicator, and separate faces for lunar date and months.

Private collection

Ridel a Paris

I recommend you to take care of the minutes:
for hours will take care of themselves

Lord Chesterfield, Letters

"Camel," Figurine Clock, Augsburg (c. 1720); base from 1750

Gilt copper; base wood (height: 26 centimeters—10¼ inches)

Delight in automatons and technical toys was still very much alive in the 18th century. This camel, driven by a little Negro boy moving a club, rolls across the table moving its mouth and eyes.

Bayerisches Nationalmuseum, Munich

Time rushes, divides, heals

Inscription on Berlin City Hall

Pocket Watch by P. L. Gautrin, Paris (1780); enameling by Jean Coteau

The face of this watch is of the very finest enameling. It shows the zodiac, the month, moon phase and lunar date, and the hours. The diamond-decorated hand revolves once every twenty-four hours.

Clockmakers Company, London

There was hardly an object into which someone did not mount a clock: hunting guns and powder horns, walking sticks, and tobacco tins for the gentlemen; fans, mirrors, or perfume bottles for the ladies. The fan is a particular masterpiece—carved of ivory, painted with mythological scenes, and adorned with gems.

Hand Mirror with Built-in Watch, England (c. 1750)

Gilt bronze, garnets, lacquer painting

Abeler Collection, Wuppertal

Fan with Built-in Watch by James Upjohn, London (c. 1755)

Painted chicken skin and ivory

Abeler Collection, Wuppertal

JUIN
JUIL.
AOUS.
SEPT.
OCTO.
NOV.
DECE.
JANV.
FEVR.
MARS.
AVRI.
MAI

Time wields a strong axe

Russian saying

Chatelaine Watch, France (c. 1790)
Gold, enamel

This watch is housed in a vase-shaped case which can also serve as a perfume vial and —like the pendant—is decorated with delicate enameling.

Württembergisches Landesmuseum, Stuttgart

Chatelaine by Roget, Paris (c. 1770)
Gold and enamel

The chain links are painted with fruit still lifes in delicate enameling; keys and seal hang from the chain next to the watch.

Omega Collection, Biel, Switzerland

Chatelaine Watch, Works by Benjamin Gray and Justin Vulliamy, London (c. 1760); case, Genevan Workmanship
Gold, enamel

It became the fashion of the 18th century to carry a watch on a chain at the belt. In valuable pieces, the watch case and chain were ornamented to match; also attached to the chain were keys and other small items—here, a good-luck charm.

Wilsdorf Collection, Rolex, Geneva

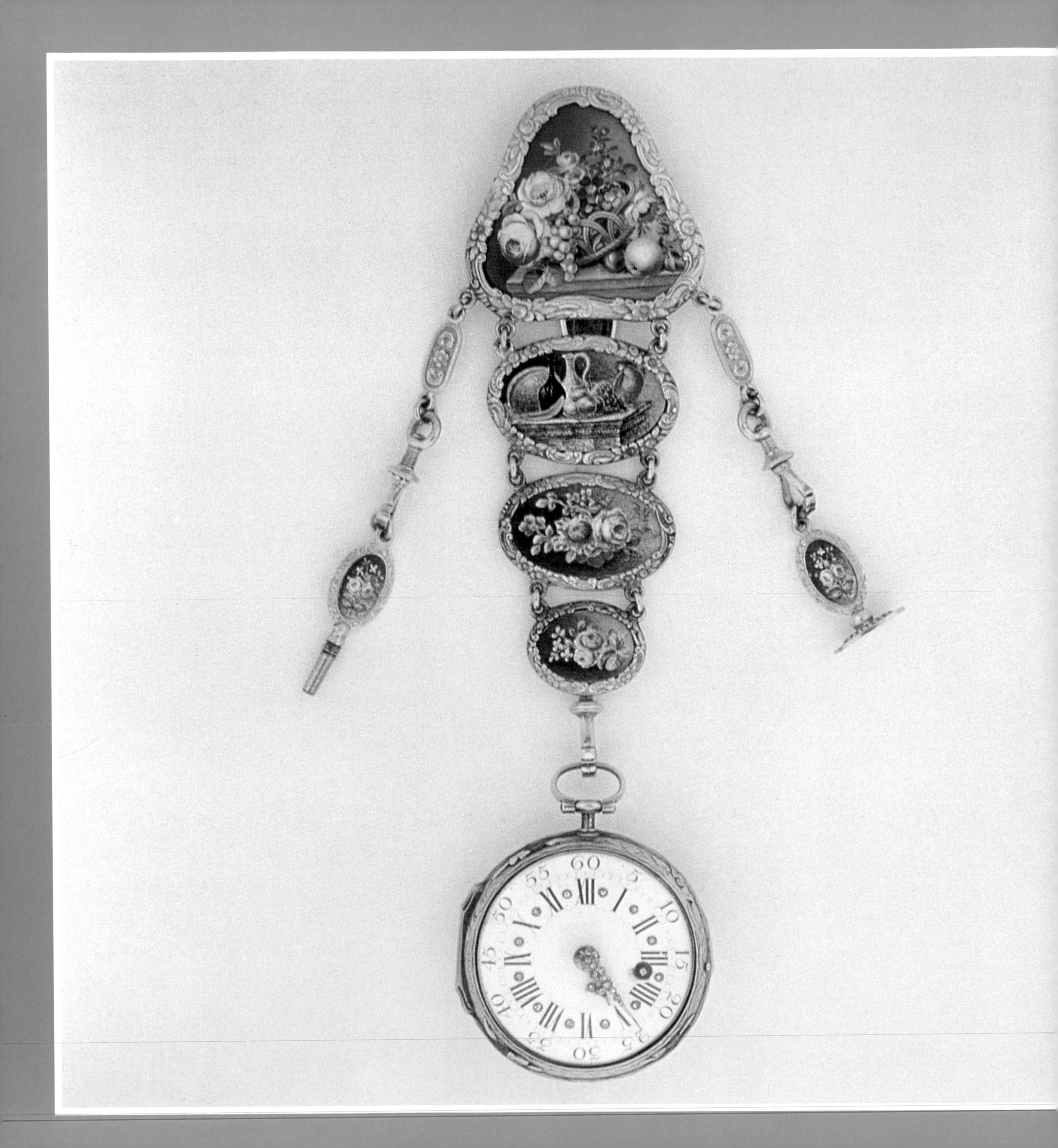

What use to you are love, luck,
education, riches,
if you begrudge yourself the time
to enjoy them at your leisure

Alexander von Gleichen-Russwurm

Pendulum Clock, France (second half of the 18th century); face by Jean Coteau

Sèvres porcelain with gilt bronze

The richly enameled face is inlaid into a frame in the shape of a lyre of blue porcelain, decorated with wonderful gilt bronze.

Louvre, Paris

He who waits for the right time may wait forever

Alfred Henderson, Latin Proverbs

Mantel Clock, Paris (c. 1810)
Gold and dark bronze

The tableau on this clock refers to the wedding of Napoleon and Marie Louise, the Austrian emperor's daughter; they are being united by a winged guardian angel.

Louvre, Paris

Pendulum Clock in Vase Shape by Thomisson, Paris (c. 1800)
Bronze, partially gilt

Württembergisches Landesmuseum, Stuttgart

Mantel Clock, marked "Thomas à Paris" (c. 1780)
Marble, gilt bronze

Two caryatids support this clock, which is crowned with cherubs playing in a bower.

Private ownership

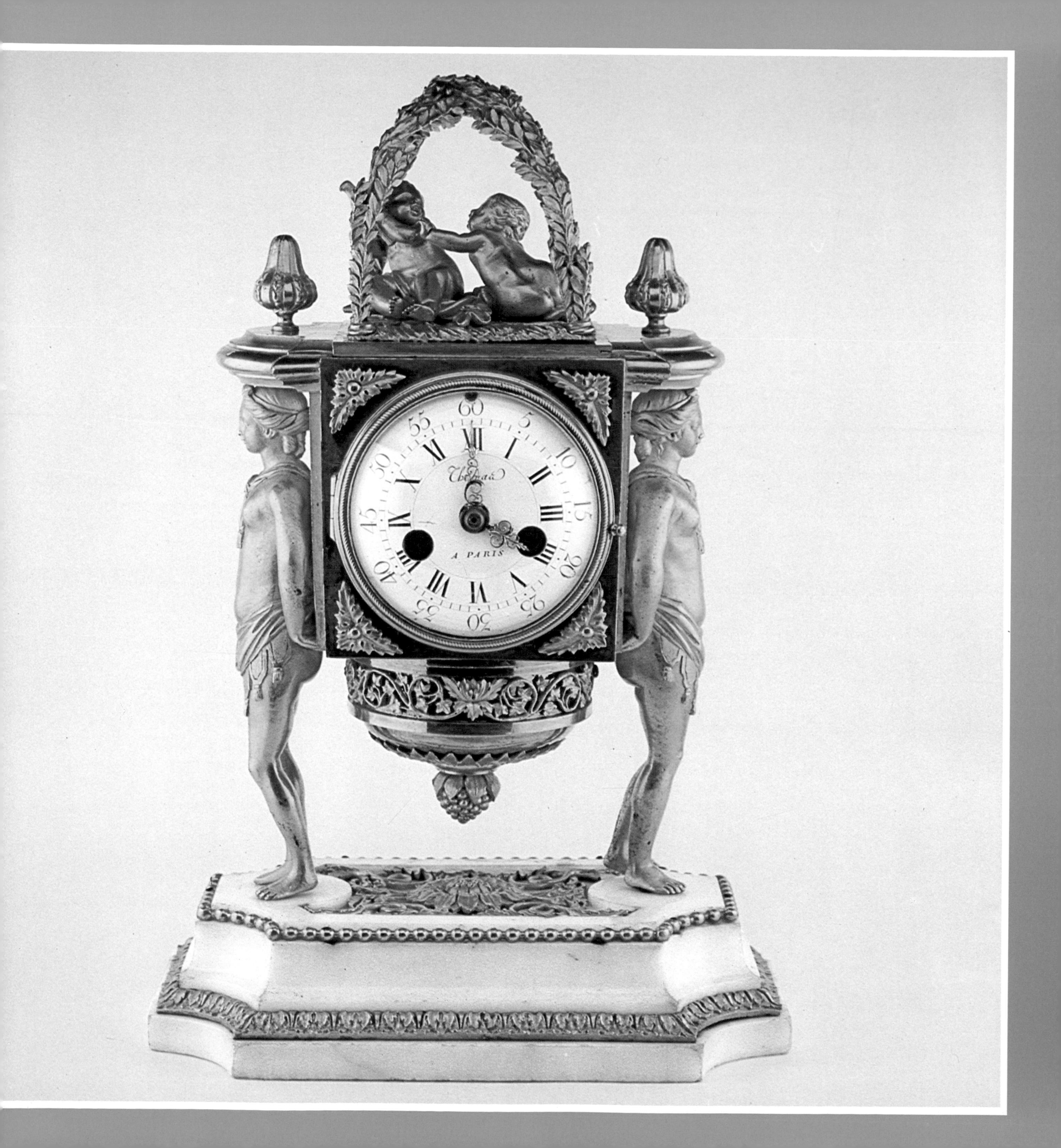
A PARIS

Time is a mighty master:
It puts much right

Pierre Corneille

Pocket Watch by Recordon & Dupont, London (c. 1800)
Gold, diamonds, and enamel

The works of this watch are of English craftsmanship; the precious case with the large diamond rosette and a harbor landscape painted on enamel comes from a Geneva workshop.

Wilsdorf Collection, Rolex, Geneva

Pocket Watch by Ferdinand Berthoud, Paris (end of the 18th century)
Gold, pearls, enamel painting

A dog flushing geese from their nest is the enamel painting motif on the watch lid.

Musée des Arts Décoratifs, Paris

Pocket Watch, Works by William Ilbery, London (c. 1800); case, Geneva
Gold, enamel, and pearls

This watch case, too, comes from one of the Geneva workshops which did a great deal of work for London clockmakers. The scene shows Oedipus and Antigone.

Wilsdorf Collection, Rolex, Geneva

Mine are not the years which time has ta'en from me,
Mine are not the years which may perhaps yet be;
The moment—that is mine; if it be what I heed,
Then that which years, eternity, has made is mine

Andreas Gryphius

Pendulum Clock, France (c. 1775)

Gilt bronze, painted Sèvres porcelain (height: 59.5 centimeters—23½ inches)

A particularly popular combination in clocks in the France of the second half of the 18th century was colorfully painted Sèvres porcelain with gilt bronze. Since a show clock belonged to the furnishings of every formal room, a plethora of clocks appeared, in every shape and size, decorated with figurines, often fitted with rich indicators like this clock with hands for days of the week and month.

The Metropolitan Museum of Art, New York (Gift of the Samuel H. Kress Foundation, 1958)

Time is the nurse and breeder of all good

William Shakespeare, Two Gentlemen of Verona

Small Table Clock, Geneva (beginning of the 19th century)

Gold enamel, porcelain, pearls (height: 20.5 centimeters—8⅛ inches)

This vase-shaped clock, richly decorated with enamel, has a music box in its base. Venus and Amor are shown in the medallion on the back.

Wilsdorf Collection, Rolex, Geneva

Musical Drum Clock, Geneva (beginning of the 19th century)

Gold enamel

A pocket watch and a music mechanism with five bells are mounted in the enamel-and-pearl-decorated drum.

Omega Collection, Biel, Switzerland

Needle Case with Watch, Geneva (beginning of the 19th century)

Gold enamel

Museo Poldi Pezzoli, Milan

Harp with Watch and Chimes, Geneva (beginning of the 19th century)

Gold enamel

These watches are examples of delight in small things; artists knew how to make them both precious and useful.

Museo Poldi Pezzoli, Milan

Time occasionally helps even the physician

Estonian saying

Genevan enamel painting reached its peak in the years just before and after 1800. The magnificent large flower still lifes, some framed by pearls, which were characteristic of Geneva, appeared at that time. Though foreign works—primarily by English clockmakers—were used to begin with, native clockmaking began to come into its own as the century progressed.

Matching Pair of Decorative Watches, Works by William Ilbery, London (end of the 18th century)
Gold, enamel, pearls

Watch with Flower Painting, Geneva (beginning of the 19th century)
Gold enamel

Watch with Enamel Painting and Pearls, Works and Case Geneva (beginning of the 19th century)
Enamel painting with flowers and fruit still life, framed by 750 pearls

Watch with Enamel Painting and Pearls, Works and Case Geneva (beginning of the 19th century)

Watch with Enamel Painting and Pearls, Works and Case Geneva (first quarter of the 19th century)

Wilsdorf Collection, Rolex, Geneva

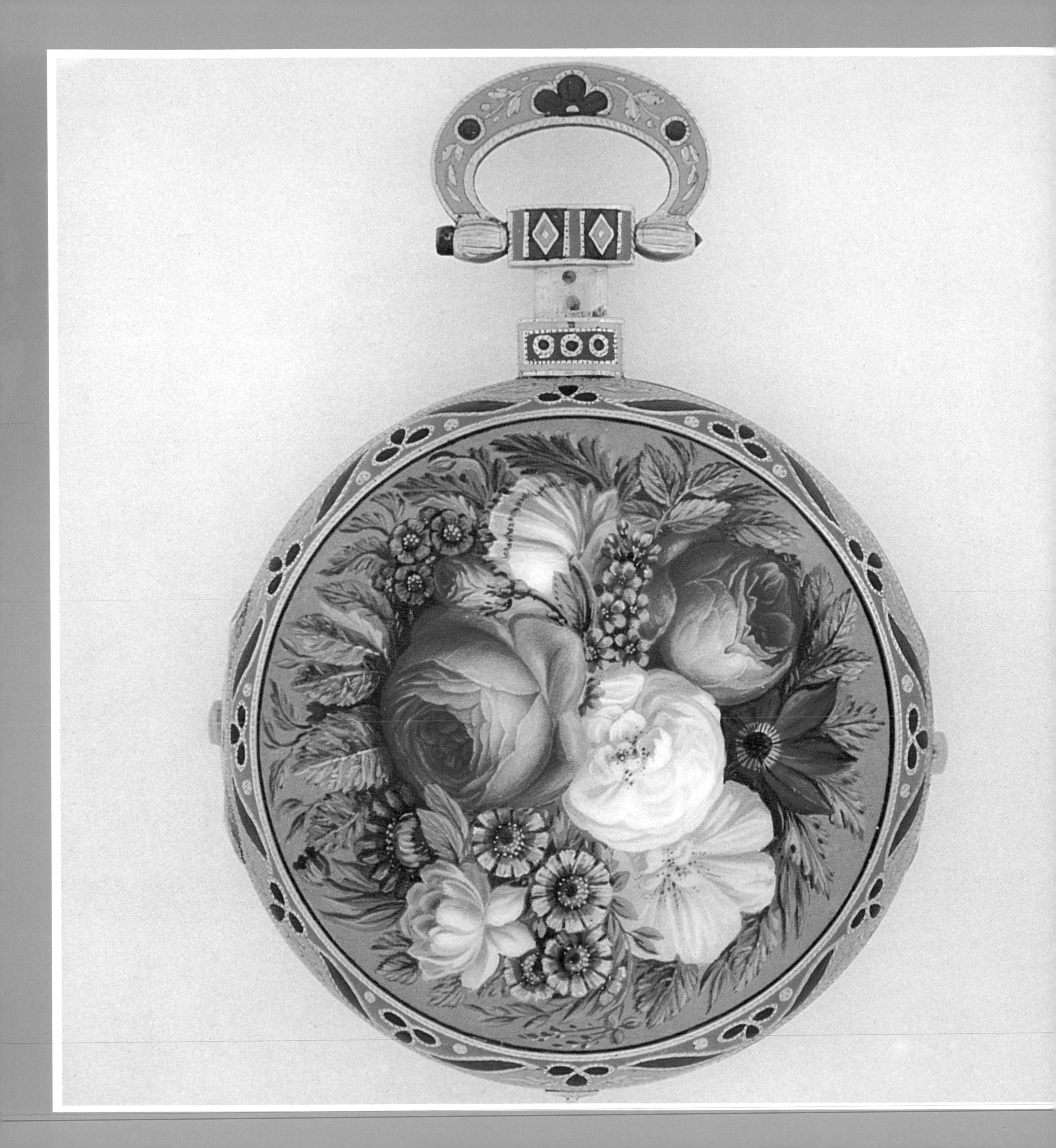

Time is one's best friend, teaching best of all the wisdom of silence

A. B. Alcott, Table Talk: "Learning"

Pocket watches with automaton figures were particularly popular at the beginning of the 19th century, and were made in great numbers, primarily in French Switzerland. At first Jacquemarts—moving figures—on the dial seemed to strike the hours; later, completely moving scenes were built into the backs of the watches.

Repeater Watch by Courvoisier et Cie., La Chaux de Fonds (beginning of the 19th century)

Gold and enamel

A woman on the balcony accompanies the striking mechanism with her movements.

Repeater Watch, probably Geneva (beginning of the 19th century)

Gold and enamel

When the ring is pressed to start the music, the five figures move in front of the scenery and seem to produce the sounds by striking the bells.

Automaton Watch, Geneva (beginning of the 19th century)

Gold and enamel

The entire scene begins to move when the ring is pressed—the dog in the treadmill turns the spit, the spinning wheel turns, and the well begins to flow.

Museo Poldi Pezzoli, Milan

Irresistible, time rushes off—
It seeks the perpetual.
Be but true, and you lay fetters eternal on it

Friedrich Schiller, The Unchangeable

The Frenchman Abraham Louis Bréguet is considered the most important clockmaker of all time. His clocks became masterpieces, often highly intricate, through a great number of technical improvements and inventions.

Traveling Clock by Abraham Louis Bréguet, Paris (c. 1810)
Case of gold bronze (height: 18 centimeters—7⅛ inches)

The front of this extremely complicated clock shows seconds; lunar date; alarm; time equation; wind-up indicator; day, date, month, and year; and temperature.

Ashmolean Museum, Oxford University (former Mollet Collection)

Pocket Watch by Abraham Louis Bréguet, Paris (c. 1785)
Multicolored gold and enamel

When the striking mechanism is released—this can also be repeated by pressing the catch—the couple next to the face and the cherub below strike the bells.

Wilsdorf Collection, Rolex, Geneva

Pocket Watch by Abraham Louis Bréguet, Paris (1820–1825)
Gold and silver

This clock is a masterpiece fitted with all the technical tricks. It is a so-called Montre perpétuelle—with self-winding action, its own scale for checking spring tension, and a particularly shock-resistant escapement. Date, day, and phase of the moon are each shown on their own dials. The hour hand jumps to the full hour, the repeater mechanism strikes the hours, quarter hours, and minutes.

Wilsdorf Collection, Rolex, Geneva

REGULATEUR
A TOURBILLON
MARDI
6
JUIN
1880
FROID
TEMPERE
CHAUD

BREGUET
No. 30
DIM
LUN
MAR
MER
JEU
VEN
SAM

Tak time in time, ere time be tint,
For time will not remain

Alexander Montgomerie, The Cherrie and the Slae

Banjo Clock, America (1815)

Gilt wood, painted glass (height: 106 centimeters—41⅞ inches)

An oddly shaped wall clock decorated with colored painting showing the eagle with the flag below on the pendulum disk box.

Private collection

You may delay, but time will not

Benjamin Franklin, Poor Richard's Almanack

Clock production began in the United States at the beginning of the 19th century. Clocks from this early time of industrial production are simple but charming; many have large painted dials and plain mahogany cases.

Standing Clock by David Wood, America (c. 1800)
Mahogany (height: 81 centimeters—32 inches)
Israel Sack Collection

Standing Clock by Eli Terry and Son, Plymouth, Connecticut (c. 1818)
Various woods, glass (height: 72 centimeters—28½ inches)
Larry Coultrip Collection, Newton, Connecticut

Standing Clock by Samuel Terry, Plymouth, Connecticut (c. 1822)
Various woods, glass (height: 70 centimeters—27⅝ inches)
Larry Coultrip Collection, Newton, Connecticut

D. Wood

Time brings help;
Await it patiently
And trust the moment, too,
For something good

Friedrich Schiller, William Tell

Pocket Watch, Paris (c. 1795)
Gold and enamel

While it often was a particularly shaped object into which a clock was mounted, here the clockworks were arranged in vase shape and set into a round pocket watch.

Württembergisches Landesmuseum, Stuttgart

Pocket Watch by André Heuen, Paris (c. 1790)
Gold enamel

The back of this watch, which matches a small ladies' watch, is completely covered with a translucent peacock-eye pattern with no figurative representation.

Württembergisches Landesmuseum, Stuttgart

He that has most time has none to lose

Thomas Fuller, Gnomologia

Long-Case Clock, marked "Tiffany & Co.," America (c. 1882–1890)

(height: 263.5 centimeters—104 inches)

Equally admirable as a richly created piece of late-19th-century furniture and as a many-dialed clock with numerous indicators, this Tiffany clock is an interesting American contribution to the history of clock shapes.

The Metropolitan Museum of Art, New York (Gift of Mary J. Kingsland, 1906)

OCTOBER NOVEMBER DECEMBER JANUARY FEBRUARY MARCH APRIL
MAY JUNE JULY AUGUST

We can enlarge the millet seed tremendously;
but we cannot make one second of time into a minute, and not
into a quarter hour. That would be splendid, if it could be done!
But instead we seek to make time smaller, and we ought to
call it that, instead of: whiling away time

Georg Christoph Lichtenberg, Mixed Writings

These watches come from the collection of the firm Patek Philippe, Geneva. They not only told their prominent owners the time, but also were often mute witnesses to great historical events.

Pocket Watch from the year 1896
It belonged to Russian General Aleksei Nikolaevich Kuropatkin (1848–1925).

Pendant Watch from the year 1851
It belonged to Queen Victoria (1819–1901).

Pocket Watch from the year 1853
It belonged to Leo Tolstoy (1828–1910).

Pocket Watch from the year 1884
It belonged to Archduke Rudolf von Hapsburg (1858–1889) of Austria.

FAB. SUISSE
S. GEORGIVS EQVITVM PATRONVS

An inch of gold will not buy an inch of time

Doolittle, Chinese Vocabulary

Pendant Watch by Poitevin & Lejeune, Paris (c. 1900)
Gold and enamel

The watch as a piece of jewelry has in no way been displaced by industrial production since the second half of the 19th century; on the contrary, it took a new lease on life. Jugendstil watches, like this imaginatively made pendant watch, were particularly popular.

Württembergisches Landesmuseum, Stuttgart

Mystery Clock by Cartier, Paris (c. 1925)
Emeralds, rubies, coral, diamonds, pearls

It is the sophisticated combination of precious materials with Far Eastern motifs that is particularly charming in this watch. The works remain hidden from view.

Private collection

Mystery Clock by Cartier, Paris (c. 1925)
Diamonds, gold, rock crystal, and black enamel

Cartier created this Mystery Clock—a clock whose hands appear to move in a void. They are actually on crystal disks moved from their edges.

Private collection

Hope not, await not,
Firmly grasp the mane of time.
What is lacking seek thou not,
And delight in what is thine

Johann Kasper Lavater

The desire to tell the time from preciously made watches is surely almost as old as the history of measuring time by geared clocks. For the present, a final point to this development—individual, extravagant, futuristic shapes.

Gold Wristwatch by Chaumet, Paris

"Rainbow Watch" by Andrew Grima, London (About Time Collection of Omega)
Gold, 69 jewels, a tourmaline as the crystal

"Esmeralda" by Andrew Grima, London (About Time Collection of Omega)
A 47.77-carat emerald serves as the crystal

"Utopia" by Andrew Grima, London (About Time Collection of Omega)
A bracelet watch of white gold with rock crystal

On the Evolution of Clocks

"And as the wheels in the movement of a clock/Do turn, so that the first, to him who sees,/Doth seem to rest, the latter one to fly . . ." Dante's words from the *Divine Comedy* speak of a technical—"timely"—revolution: the invention of geared-wheel clocks with mechanical escapements. It is thus established that around 1300, the time of Dante, the alternation of day and night, which had been the basic time measurement for thousands of years, was no longer the only valid way of measuring time.

The first attempts at breaking down time were made by the Chinese and the Babylonians. They are said to have used the regularity of the sun's "revolving around the earth" for time measurement, with the help of the sun and a stone stele or a shadow staff, in the third millennium B.C. And at about the same time, there are notations in Egyptian hieroglyphics indicating that sundials were already in use there.

It is considered certain that in all advanced cultures, the same principles or similar ones were used for determining time—from the above-mentioned Egyptians, Babylonians, and Chinese through the ancient inhabitants of Greece to the natives of Central America.

Such important philosophers and mathematicians as Plato and Archimedes, too, took part in the further development of the sundial. As early as 330 B.C., a portable sundial was said to have been built by the Greek Parmenio. But even after the beginning of mechanical time measurement by geared-wheel clocks, sundials did not lose favor—they were cheaper, and they could be used for adjusting clocks.

However, the sundial did have competition relatively early—from mechanical clocks with water drive, about which we know very little. A water clock is said to have been built in Egypt as early as 1500 B.C. The Egyptian Prince Amenemhet invented it to get around the dilemma of being able to tell time only in sunshine.

Over the centuries, these early clocks achieved a certain status as unusual gifts. A king of Burgundy received two from Theodoric the Great, a sundial and a water clock. And it is said that Haroun al Raschid in A.D. 807 sent Charlemagne not only elephants but also a water clock with moving figures.

The clock tower of the Chinese scientist Su Sung is the high point in time measurement using water. The drive was a water wheel with a most ingenious escapement through a lever mechanism. The early water clocks, which showed the time by the level of the water running in or out, had little in common with this work of art aside from the basic element of water. Genghis Khan's mounted hordes destroyed it in the Mongolian Wars.

But the Greeks, too, built ever more refined time-measuring devices. Although the riddles of the mechanics of these intricate instruments—e.g. the spheres of Archimedes—have not been solved, archaeological discoveries have shown that they must have been extraordinarily complex constructions.

As to the exact time of the invention of the mechanical clock in our sense—a geared works run by weights and having an escapement—we remain as entirely in the dark as we are about the identity of the inventor.

For all that, we can set the hour of birth for the geared-wheel clock with weighted drive some time in the years preceding 1300. The first literary references come from this time.

The most famous clocks are those in the great cathedrals of France and England. The best-known is probably the one finished in 1354, the first Strasbourg Cathedral clock (the name of the builder has not come down to us). This clock, in its present construction—the third, built by Jean-Baptiste Schwilgué and finished in 1842—is a masterpiece, equipped with all the technical refinements imaginable: astronomical time data, calendar information, and moving figures. It proves, too, that the maker used extraordinary abilities in precision mechanics, and must also have been an excellent mathematician.

We must probably attribute almost all further developments in tower clocks, at first built almost entirely of iron and mostly made by deft locksmiths or gunsmiths, to such unusual combinations of great ability in handicrafts and science.

The invention of the winding spring as drive for the clockworks, in lieu of the weights which exclusively had moved clocks for more than a century, was a milestone in the history of mechanical time measurement. The first spring-drive clocks were probably made in Flanders or Burgundy. The clock belonging to Philip the Good of Burgundy is the oldest extant spring-wound clock. And now it became possible to make smaller and more showy clocks as well.

During the high flowering of the Gothic period, with its luxuriously equipped clocks and watches, only princes, nobles, cloisters, or rich cities could afford them. But with the expansion of technical knowledge, the triumphal march of the clock and watch as a general-usage timepiece was not to be stayed.

According to literary sources, the art of clockmaking was originally concentrated in Italy and Flanders. In the course of the 16th century, Nuremberg and Augsburg became clockmaking centers.

Once the spring winder had been invented, it was only a relatively small step from tower clocks, through room clocks in rich city houses, down to the clock that could be carried about. Around 1513, the chronicler Colcheus wrote that one Peter Henlein in Nuremberg was making small portable clocks with striking mechanism. These first "pocket watches" —surely nothing but a reduced form of the table clock which had just been introduced, or a further development of the traveling clock—were in the shape of a tin can or drum.

Besides further technical development, the Renaissance contributed its share to enhanced artistic clockmaking. Wenzel Jamnitzer, in Nuremberg, was probably one of the most inventive and gifted goldsmiths of the time; his works are among the most consummate and beautiful of the epoch.

The awe-inspiring automaton clocks, with moving figures and animals, which were soon coveted by all Europe, originated primarily in Augsburg. This time saw also the first clocks with divisions into minutes and seconds, with long-running movement (three months) and the first rolling-ball clocks, which promised particularly regular time measurement.

Up to this time, movement precision and regulability could not be measurably improved upon because of mechanical problems, despite many experiments with new drive regulators. Clocks were made that indicated a multiplicity of data, some of them extremely complex. Probably the most extraordinary result of these efforts is the planet orbit clock by Baldewein and Bucher—a mathematical and technical masterpiece.

Around 1637, a discovery as simple as it was ingenious—the law of the pendulum—permitted, through the pendulum's isochronism (even swing), the most comprehensive advance in the precision of time measurement. Galileo Galilei had conceived the idea as he observed a ceiling lamp swinging in the Cathedral of Pisa. Old and blind, in 1641 he gave his son Vincenzio instructions for making a pendulum clock. Vincenzio built it, then destroyed it for fear of the authorities, remembering only too well his father's exile and indictment for heresy because of his discoveries.

Pioneering though Galileo's discovery may have been, the real inventor of the pendulum clock is a Dutchman, Christian Huygens. In 1656, with his first pendulum clock, he laid the cornerstone for this type of clock and for its drive precision, while Galileo's result was actually a sort of swing measurement.

The pendulum could not, of course, be used for portable watches. Huygens invented the spiral spring for these. This in turn resulted in a tremendous upsurge of pocket-watch production, centered in France and Switzerland.

Following this, a multiplicity of shapes developed. Campanus, an Italian, made a clock for Pope Alexander VII; its numerals were illuminated from the back by a small lamp, and could thus be read even at night. Cross-shaped pocket watches were made, and small watches in the shape of death's-heads were particularly popular; they were supposed to remind their bearers not only of passing time, but also of the ephemerality of all things earthly.

The introduction of the pendulum also resulted in a changed case shape; instead of the Renaissance clock, with many viewing sides, clocks as we have them now, with one "front" side, developed. Pendulum clocks appeared in various countries in numerous special shapes. Decoration and artistic appearance often were more important than the technical inner life of the clock. For example, the French carpenter André Boulle, working at the end of the 17th century, built long-case clocks of extraordinary beauty. He laid silver or brass plates and tortoiseshell on top of each other and sawed them out following patterns drawn on them. Not only wall clocks, but even more so standing clocks, made in England as early as 1600, expressed French showiness in all its variety through precious inlay work and imaginative case shapes. There were, indeed, clockmakers in other countries who produced pendulum clocks, often with very complex mechanisms; but the pendulum and standing clocks made in France for the King and nobles have not been surpassed in elegance and magnificence.

Besides the rich variety of shapes in standing clocks, two developments of the 17th century are particularly noteworthy; first was the invention of the balance by the Dutch Huygens. In Paris in 1674, he had the first clock with balance and spiral spring made. All wearable watches of today function on this same principle. And second was a new enameling technique for small objects, developed by Jean Toutin. A thin coat of paint was put, with a paintbrush, on a layer of previously fired white enamel, and fixed there by another firing. The technique lent the enamel picture an incomparable transparency. Toutin lived in England, where he painted his wonderful portraits of rulers and highly placed personalities on surfaces hardly larger than 1¼ inches square. Small wonder that this artistic decorative element was adopted in fashioning valuable watches.

For a long time, the most important center for pocket-watch production was Blois, France. After 1685 (repeal of the Edict of Nantes), many of the clockmakers living there, as well as enamel painters and goldsmiths, fled to Switzerland, making Geneva the second center of enamel painting and clockmaking. The Huguenot Pierre Huaud and his three sons, having lived in Geneva since 1630, received Swiss citizenship in 1671. Even today, the unusual artistic gift of the enamel-painting Huaud family can be seen in the portraits and landscapes of extraordinary beauty and delicacy, painted on pocket watches. Two of the sons, Jean-Pierre and Ami, worked in Berlin from 1686 to 1700 for Friedrich Wilhelm, the "Great Elector," who wished to establish a state clockmaking industry.

After this, pocket watches were decorated not only by enamel painting; the finest engraving, pearls, and precious stones were added. Around 1700, one of the final decisive improvements was perfected by the Genevan mathematician Nicolas Facio, living in England. He found a way to bore rubies. One of the biggest problems was solved by this: The metal seats used up to that time for all moving parts had to be lubricated with oil, which often produced verdigris. Polished steel seats were also sometimes used, but there was energy loss through friction with these, and they wore out.

The procedure of using bored rubies as seats, registered by Facio for English patent in 1704, gave the geared wheel and balance much greater accuracy of movement, and also permitted reduction of drive strength. English clockmakers succeeded in keeping secret the production procedure for these "clock stones" for almost seventy years. The first use of rubies outside England is attributed to the Frenchman Ferdinand Berthoud, who delivered two extremely exact marine timepieces to the French Admiralty and received a title and pension for it.

Indeed, England had played a leading role in the development and production of clocks for quite a long time. Among other things invented by English clockmakers: anchor escapement (Dr. Robert Hooke), cylinder escapement (Thomas Tompion), and mercurial compensation for pendulums (George Graham).

In 1761, John Harrison succeeded in his life's work, mastering the problem of determining geographical longitude. His "Timekeeper No. 4" varied only five seconds on a voyage to Jamaica lasting 161 days. For this he received a prize of 20,000 pounds sterling from the British government. English clockmaking had earned great prestige and Harrison won the competition against the other entrants. Reaching this goal—the greatest possible precision in ships' clocks, as requested by the British Admiralty—was, in the truest sense of the word, a race against time.

Toward the end of the 18th century, the Frenchman Abraham Louis Bréguet used ruby or sapphire seats, first imported from England and later produced in France, for his famed "subscription watches." In many ways he was a brilliant technician. The invention of the pocket watch with second hand, the improvement of automatic winding, and the invention of shock absorption for the axle seat of the balance—besides many other new achievements—made the reputation of the Bréguet clockmaking dynasty. Their pocket watches are masterpieces of technical precision. The first super-flat pocket watches were also made by Bréguet. In him, his contemporaries, and his successors, special clock mechanisms reached the acme of perfection.

As the "empire" style started to go out of fashion, clocks shaped like flowers, hearts, and mandolins were highly prized by society women. About 1800—the second flowering of Genevan enamel painting—wonderful pocket watches were created, especially for the Chinese trade. "Old clock" cases (cases had long since been technically perfect) experienced a last artistic flowering (so far) in the Jugendstil period.

Regarding our own time's decorative preferences, the external shape of the clock has also changed; but the desire to tell time from "enchanting cases" remains with us. Besides producing for the mass market, jewelers and some of the larger clockmaking firms still take pleasure in heeding individual wishes by designing exclusive models.

From about the middle of the last century, industrial production took over more and more in all areas of clockmaking. What had for centuries been a basic condition for any progress—the scientific pioneer spirit, the technical drive to explore, and an artistic gift coupled with a joy in craftsmanship—had to make way for economical production methods and commercial production decisions.

Emigrants built the first clock factories in America, affording a stimulus and a necessity for European clockmakers to adopt their production methods.

And the clock became a mass-market commodity.

Yet time did not stand still. Enormous technical advances led to new systems in clockmaking. Thus, besides battery-operated electrical clocks, there are now electronic clocks, quartz clocks which show the time without a single moving mechanical part, and the atomic clock. Even if these time measurement systems technically have nothing more to do with the "most beautiful clocks" shown in this book, the atomic clock, as a momentary endpoint to development, does embody, with its almost absolute exactitude, that same wish to determine time which first tempted that unknown-to-us master to dream up the first geared-wheel clock.

And it certainly is not a yearning for yesteryear which makes these "mechanical aides to time" so very desirable to the collector; it is the deep fascination issuing from these milestones in the history of time measurement (be they but the smallest milestones)—from these "enchanting cases of time."